RECIPES AND TEXT BY LAURA ARENDSEN ROWE

PHOTOGRAPHY BY AUDREY SCHWIMMER

DESIGN BY MIRA LANCASTER

ISBN-13: 978-1453876824 ISBN-10: 1453876820

Kathleen, So glad you love the book! Enjoy!!! Laura MAY 2015

LAURA ARENDSEN ROWE

This book is dedicated to my grandma Lizl, who taught me to make Linzertorte,
to my grandma Gert, who taught me to make raspberry jam,
to my dad who endured my childhood fascination with Jell-o brand gelatin desserts,
to my sisters who trade for their favorite cookies at Christmas,
to my mother who told me I could be a chef
before I even knew such a profession existed
and to Jeff Rowe for all of his love and support.

Many thanks to everyone who has ever shared a recipe with me
and to all those who have been kind enough to let me try new things on them.
Thank you for allowing me to bake for you.

A special thank you to my photographer, Audrey Schwimmer, for helping me
with this project; thank you for making everything look good enough to eat!
Many thanks to my graphic designer, Mira Lancaster, for helping me
shape the recipes and photographs into a book.
Thanks to Julie Christofferson for her input,
and thanks to Stasia Poncher for indexing the book.
Many thanks to everyone who helped with recipe testing and marketing.

Thank you for purchasing this book.

A portion of the proceeds from its sale supports
southeastern Michigan's largest food bank, Food Gatherers.

When I was about ten years old I used to visit my grandparents for a week or two in the summer. My mother's parents were German and my father's were Dutch-Danish. I loved to cook and, luckily, so did both my grandmothers. One summer, my Dutch-Danish grandmother, Grandma Gert, taught me to make raspberry jam with fresh raspberries from my Grandpa Bert's garden. (Yes, they really were Bert and Gert.) The following week I went from her house to my Grandma Lisl's house where we used the raspberry jam to make Linzertorte. My Grandma Lisl was German and she baked using a gram measure and a scale. I converted the metric measurements for the recipe into cups and teaspoons, etc. and have kept that recipe and others from her for years. No one, myself included, could bake like my Grandma Lisl.

Throughout my childhood and teens I was always in the kitchen when I had free time. I scoured Better Homes and Gardens magazines for recipes with my baby sister in my lap playing a game we called, "That Looks Good" and tore out pages with recipes for later use. My mother always worried that I would try something which would not turn out and that I would be disappointed. She still talks about some triple braided anise seed bread that I made. She was sure it would fail to rise or fall or just fail in general, but it was fine. I never worried about things not turning out. I am sure that I had my share of failures or goofs, but nothing could keep me out of the kitchen for long.

I can still remember being in our kitchen one day when my mother said to me, "You know, you could be a chef." I thought time stood still. "People would pay you to cook," she went on. I was probably only about thirteen years old and until then I had only thought of cooking as this thing I loved to do. The only possibilities I had thought of for the answer to, "What do you want to be when you grow up?" were the traditional "lawyer" or "doctor." I had no idea there were other creative options out there. It was a watershed moment in my life. From then on my answer was, "I want to be a chef."

Life is full of compromises. When the time came for me to go to college, I still loved to cook, but it was inevitable that I would go to college for some type of professional degree before trying out the culinary arts. I struck a bargain with my father and agreed that if I went to the University of Michigan and finished, he would also send me through culinary school. At the time, I was applying for the culinary program at Schoolcraft College in Livonia, Michigan, and the wait to get into the program was four years, so it seemed that everything would work out fine. After two years at Michigan and a lot of indecision regarding a major, my name came to the top of the list for Schoolcraft's Culinary Arts program. Additional negotiations with my father yielded the result that I would defer and stay at Michigan to finish up and I settled on a degree in business administration. The fall after graduation I started the two-year program in the culinary arts. The instructors were a colorful set of characters and all very talented. I was instantly enamored of the pastry chef, Chef Steck. He had been the pastry chef at a hotel in downtown Detroit for many years and was a very precise and disciplined man with a wonderful sense of humor. I still love to quote his favorite admonition to us: "Remember, strain the mixture, don't strain yourself." Sometimes I try it out on my staff, but they just look at me funny; I am not sure it translates out of the kitchen and into the office. Chef Steck taught two semesters on pastry: one on baking and the other on frosting and filling, including decorating. It was wonderful. We learned all about production baking and we made the best macaroon cookies. We always had to taste the product, of course, so we would know how things turned out.

While in school another chef, Chef Benson, helped me find a job with a small catering and specialty foods shop in West Bloomfield. I worked for a fellow graduate of the Schoolcraft culinary program, Debbie Hamilton, and her partner, Patrick Vargo, who both had worked for a famous restaurant in Detroit before starting their own business. I baked and worked the front counter doing sales. I learned a lot of new recipes and had fun trying out new things for the shop. Debbie taught me to make trifle, which we would sell by the pint. Our favorite was the Coconut Macaroon Trifle and I think we made it more for ourselves than for the customers. I have changed the recipe since then, using almond cake instead of ladyfingers.

After graduating from culinary school I moved back to Ann Arbor and eventually found a position as an assistant pastry chef at Weber's Inn. The pastry chef at Weber's was a former Culinary Institute of America graduate. I learned to bake in very large quantities there. We made French bread and Danish pastry from scratch. We made sheet cakes and pies for banquets, and fine pastries and tortes for the dining room. We even made wedding cakes. It was really something. At Thanksgiving we would bake over 200 pumpkin pies, and that was just one of 6 pastries being offered that day. Flour came in 80# bags. It was heaven. After about a year, the current pasty chef decided to get married and move to Virginia, so I became the head pastry chef.

We had begun to try a lot of new things already, but now I was very interested in making the best pastries from scratch, given the volume that was needed in the hotel. I remember that once a salesman came in with some instant mousse powder, just add whipped cream, etc. I would not even try it. He stormed off in a huff. I wanted everything to be as homemade as possible. Even in 1988 the culinary field was changing and many companies were starting to sell pre-made frozen desserts to restaurants. Weber's Inn was one of the few family-owned hotels which still had its own bakeshop and I wanted to take advantage of the opportunity to keep the art of baking alive. I had a crew of four and we baked day and night.

Before becoming head pastry chef at Weber's Inn, I had taken a course in advance pastry at Washtenaw Community College, to add to my general knowledge base of recipes, and when the instructor left I was offered the job of teaching the course myself. I taught two semesters of an advanced pastry class at Washtenaw Community College in Ypsilanti, Michigan. As a final exam I would have my students create a new pastry recipe by combining the recipes they had learned in class. While writing this book I ran across a few of their exams. One student made French Meringue Shells, placed a small amount of chocolate Ganache in the bottom and then topped it with Lemon Curd and Whipped Cream – touché! I liked teaching and began to think about it as an alternative career, at the same time feeling the pull toward a life with more regular hours and less time on my feet. I decided to go back to school for a degree in the fine arts and education. I finished up the degree in fine arts, but obtained a job in event sales and soon found myself on my way to another career I had never imagined existed, the world of event planning. For a few years I made wedding cakes while I worked full-time in event sales for Katherine's Catering and Special Events, Inc. Though I have wandered even further away from baking into the field of institutional advancement, event planning is still a portion of my work today.

At the time I began writing this book, the majority of my baking took the form of what to make for someone's birthday or, of course, the annual cookie baking marathon that comprises my December weekends. My decision to write this book came because I was looking for a recipe in my old binder of recipes, many of which we used at the hotel, and found that my recipe pages were turning yellow and the ink was actually fading away. 20 years of sitting on the shelf and my beloved, hand-written recipes were fading into oblivion! My friend, Audrey Schwimmer, agreed to be my photographer and we started the book by doing our first photo shoot at the Zen Buddhist Temple in Ann Arbor, Michigan. It was the annual 2008 potluck for Buddha's Birthday celebration and I made Carrot Cake, Raspberry Rhapsody, Flourless Chocolate Mousse Cake, Gluten-Free Chocolate Chocolate Chip Zucchini Cake and Coconut Macaroon Trifle, plus some cookies. From there I have been baking a few things at a time and getting together with my faithful photographer to amass this collection of recipes from my childhood and time as a pastry chef. I have included ways to make some of these pastries gluten-free or with alternative natural sweeteners, such as maple syrup. I also include a recipe for Gluten-Free Baking Mix which can be substituted for flour. Writing this book has rekindled my love for baking and I have rediscovered that spark of enthusiasm for the craft which I loved as a child. I know there are others out there like me. So, I have started the blog BakingPureandSimple.blogspot.com. Please visit the site for additional recipes and baking lore. Let me know if you come up with any new combinations from the recipes in this book, like my students did for their final exams.

I hope you will enjoy these recipes. I wrote this book so that they would not be lost but would be available for those who love to bake as much as I do. They come from as far back as my earliest memory of baking with my grandmothers and from as professional a situation as the kitchen we had in the hotel. Some of these recipes take more than a little time to prepare; others are simple with only a few ingredients. No matter which you choose to try, I hope you will enjoy preparing them as much as you enjoy tasting and serving them.

Baking Pure & Simple

Table of Contents

Good to Know

Recipes

About Ingredients

Always use fresh, high quality ingredients. It's the key to how things will taste. Every now and then I go through my cupboards and check things. I taste nuts, flours, and chocolate, just to make sure nothing has spoiled. You may not feel that you would know if the nuts or flour was spoiled but here is the thing: if it has been in the cupboard for over 6 months, or you cannot remember when you bought it or it tastes bitter at all or the expiration date has passed, then in all likelihood it is time to toss it. Look at it this way: if you use it and it is old then chances are whatever you make with it will taste off. With dry goods it will probably not make anyone sick, but still, why spend all that energy and risk your reputation as a baker just to save a few pennies?

There is a saying in the food industry:

"When in doubt, throw it out!"

Butter: Use unsalted butter for baking, period. Unsalted butter is the preferred choice for baking and has been forever. If you must substitute margarine, try to find unsalted margarine for baking.

Chocolate: Use a high quality semi-sweet 52.9% cocoa dark chocolate. I like to use Callebaut chocolate. It comes in 11-pound blocks, and I usually purchase half a block. We have a shop called "By The Pound" in Ann Arbor and I can get it there. You may have to find a specialty or bulk food store to purchase a whole or half block. Usually you can find 1 to 2-pound blocks at specialty grocery stores.

Cocoa: Use Dutched cocoa whenever possible.

Eggs: Use large eggs. Use real eggs, not egg substitutes. Consuming raw or undercooked eggs may increase your risk of foodborne illness. A few of my recipes contain uncooked eggs. I have been making them for years without any problems. I do, however, offer alternative preparations for those recipes which do not require uncooked eggs.

Flour: Use the right kind of flour for the recipe. All purpose flour has gluten in it and cake flour does not. This gluten gives bread its dense and chewy texture. In many cases all purpose flour is the right flour to use, but if the recipe calls for cake flour be sure to use cake flour. The quantities do not always equate if substitutions are made. When substituting alternate grain flours because of allergies to wheat, see the Gluten-Free Baking Mix recipe below.

Heavy Cream: Heavy cream is the same thing as whipping cream.

Lemon or Orange Juice: Use real lemon juice squeezed from fresh lemons. To get the most juice per lemon make sure the lemons are room temperature, then cut them in half. Use a fork to break up the pulp and squeeze the juice through a strainer to remove the seeds. Or if you are lucky enough to have a juicer, that works, too. I have a manual juicer, which is a good work out for your upper arms. Remember to switch sides.

Vanilla: Use real vanilla. Imitation vanilla tastes artificial and has an aftertaste. I think it is better to just leave out the vanilla rather than use artificial vanilla.

Gluten-Free Baking Mix

If you can find a good gluten-free baking mix that you like then by all means use the commercial product. I have found these gluten-free mixes to be very good. You can also make your own gluten-free mixture using the following ingredients. Make a batch and keep it on hand. In general you can substitute this one-to-one for white or whole wheat flour. Sometimes you may need to add a little more of the baking mix. Combine all ingredients and store in an air-tight container. Makes 5 cups.

1 cup coconut flour
1 cup potato starch
1 cup tapioca flour
1 cup sweet white sorghum flour
1 cup amarath flour

Alternative Sweeteners

My favorite alternative sweetener is maple syrup. Be sure you are buying pure maple syrup. I found out the hard way that just because the label says maple syrup does not mean that the bottle contains anything that came out of a tree! Check the ingredient list. When substituting maple syrup for sugar in cookies, I find that you can reduce the amount of eggs by half and that you may need to add more dry ingredients such as another cup of oats or a half cup more flour. Other liquid sweeteners such as agave and honey would need the same accommodations. I have not tried all the new artificial sweeteners on the market as I like to stay with natural ingredients as much as possible.

About Equipment

This section could go on forever. Therefore, I have limited it to items which most people may not already have in their kitchen. You may be familiar with some of these items if you have been baking for awhile. I did not include the description of a pie pan, a rolling pin or a cake pan as I believe these things are in common use.

Bench Scraper: A bench scraper is a metal rectangle with a hard rubber handle on one side. It is used to scrape down the baking woodblock or "bench" after making bread or other yeast dough It is also great for dividing dough.

Cake Cardboard: These are round pieces of corrugated cardboard which can be purchased in various sizes corresponding to the sizes of cake pans. They can be cut down to the proper size if they are too big. They are used to hold the cake while you are working on it.

Cake Combs: Triangular metal tool with serrated edges used to decorate the sides of cakes.

Cake Turntable: Cake turntables consist of a round, usually metal top about 14" in diameter which fits into a base so that it can turn, just like a record turn table. The idea is that you can put your cake on the turntable and ice and decorate it while easily moving it from side to side. If you don't have one you will just have to turn the surface your cake is on while working on it. I did not have a turntable while working on this book, so I do not mention it much in the instructions. I wanted to be sure you could put together all of these tortes and cakes without one, and you can. It is easier to work on your cake on a turntable, so if you plan to bake a lot, or just like to have all the right gadgets, pick one up.

Handheld Spatula: This is a kidney or rectangular shaped spatula which does not have a handle. You can use it to fold ingredients together, especially when folding in egg whites for mousses. The other kind of rubber spatula works fine, too, if you don't like to get your hands dirty.

Icing Spatula: This is a fairly long - usually about 12 inches - metal spatula with a wooden or plastic handle. It is about an inch and a half wide. The length makes it easier to smooth out large surfaces in as few strokes as possible.

Long Serrated Knife: The average serrated knife is about 8 inches long. The longer version can be as much as 14 inches long. It is great for splitting cake layers, though a shorter knife will work as well.

About Equipment

[Continued from page 9]

Mixer Attachments: I am fortunate to have a 4½ quart Kitchen-Aid brand mixer. In fact I have two, one I have barely ever used, since the one I have had and used for 21 years is still going strong. No matter what brand of mixer you have it will likely have attachments. I will refer to 3 through out the book.

Dough Hook: The dough hook is just as it sounds. It looks like a single hook with a flat area at the top where it attaches to the machine. The flat area on top stops the dough from climbing up into the mixer. The dough hook is primarily used for making bread.

Paddle: The paddle is a flat, single-blade attachment which has a few bars through the center and is used for creaming ingredients, such as butter, cream cheese, etc.

Whip or Whisk: The whisk is made of metal wires and looks like a hand whisk except it is the size and shape of the bowl it is made for. It is used for whipping cream, whole eggs, whites, yolks, genoise style cake batter or buttercream.

Pastry Bag: Pastry bags are used to hold whipped cream or buttercream for piping as decoration. Generally the pastry bag is fitted with a pastry tip. I like to substitute a plastic freezer bag (with the corner cut out for the pastry tip) for a commercial store bought pastry bag. It may take a few freezer bags before you get the size of the corner cut just right so that your pastry tip does not slide right through, but the advantage is that you can have a clean pastry bag every time. Another advantage is that it is bigger than the commercial pastry bag so you will not have to refill it in order to finish decorating.

Pastry Tip: There are many different types of pastry tips. For the purpose of this book I use the larger versions, about 2 inches long. Smaller tips need to be fitted into a coupler, which definitely needs to be used with a commercial pastry bag. The larger versions I like to use work very well with the plastic freezer bag substitute.

Round tip: I generally use a round tip for other types of decorating which require a smooth round circle. Examples of this include a small ¼ inch diameter round tip as for decorating the Cherry Dacquoise or a larger ½ inch diameter for piping Mousse into serving dishes or for piping Pâte à Choux into circles for Paris Breast. For the larger size, I just carefully cut the whole in the corner of the freezer bag and omit the tip. This gives me total control over the size of the hole.

Star or Fluted Tip: This will have a fluted opening and will produce flowerets or swirls for decorating around the top of a cake.

Tart Pans with Removable Bottoms: Most fluted tart pans have removable bottoms. The advantage is that once your tart is finished you can remove the sides, showing off the beauty of the fluted crust, while not disturbing the bottom of the tart. This is very advantageous for serving and cutting. If you bring a tart somewhere without your outer rim, be sure you remember to get the bottom back before leaving. I have several orphaned outer tart shell rims.

Removing Cakes from Pans

Always allow the cake layers to cool completely before removing. To remove a cake, run a metal spatula or non-serrated knife around the edge of the cake, then place the bottom of the cake pan over a hot stove burner for about 20 to 30 seconds, turning slowly and constantly. Using a hot pad to hold the pan, invert the cake pan over a flat cake cardboard the same size as the pan. Tap firmly on a wooden cutting board turning by 90 degrees each time until the cake comes loose. Re-apply heat if the cake does not come free easily.

Splitting Cakes Horizontally

Place the cake on a flat surface, either a serving plate without a lip or a cake cardboard. If you have a cake turntable it is helpful to use it. Using a long serrated knife, slice the cake from the side toward the center about 2 inches in. Leaving the knife in place turn the cake and continue slicing and turning until you reach the point where you started. Move the knife further in toward the center of the cake and continue around the cake again, repeating until you cut through at the center.

Assembling Cakes

To assemble cakes with icing or filling between the layers you will need an icing spatula and either a serving platter or a cake cardboard. Using a cake cardboard is good because you can get all the icing on the cake before placing it on the final serving platter. This will help you have a clean presentation for your final cake or torte. Check the size of the cake cardboard. If it is bigger than your cake layer cut it down to the right size. Place the cake layer upside down on the cake cardboard and then place it on a flat surface such as a cutting board or cake turntable if you have one. Check the instructions for the torte you are making and if it is necessary to moisten the layers with simple syrup or liqueur than follow the instructions for moistening the layers in the recipe. Next, place approximately ¾ cup to 1 cup of the filling or icing on the layer and spread it out to within ¼ inch of the edge of the cake. The layer of icing should be about ¼ inch thick. Place the next layer squarely on top of the filling and continue this pattern if there are additional layers. Do not place filling on the top layer but proceed with icing instructions.

Icing Cakes

If you have a cake turntable it is helpful to use it. Using the metal icing spatula, always begin by spreading icing on the top of the cake and bringing it out to the edge. Next spread icing on the sides and up just over the top edge of the cake. Carefully flatten or scrape the icing toward the center of the top at a 90 degree angle from the side of the cake to make a crisp corner edge. Each time pull the spatula over the top of the cake from just beyond the edge toward the center, keeping your spatula edge evenly horizontal at the level of the top of the cake. If the cake is dark in color and the icing is light you may want to put on a "crumb layer" of icing. To do this cover the entire cake in a very thin layer of icing and then go back over the cake with the rest of the icing, making a thicker outer layer. The inner layer seals in the crumbs so that the outer layer is nice and clean. Run the icing spatula under the edge of the cake all around the bottom to cleanly release the icing from the surface you are working on before removing the cake.

Have your final serving platter ready and nearby. If you are applying nuts or shaved chocolate to the sides of your cake have them ready in a pile on a dinner size plate. Slide your icing spatula under the cake cardboard at the bottom of the cake. Gently lift the spatula enough to get your hand under the cake and support the cake with your palm while you apply small handfuls of nuts or chocolate shavings to the sides over the pile, allowing the excess to fall back onto the plate. Once the cake is covered transfer it to the final serving platter. If you are not applying any covering simply lift the cake as indicated directly onto the serving platter. In either case be sure you have the cake centered on the platter before you lower it down completely. As you lower the cake reinsert the cake spatula between your palm and the cake cardboard and then remove your hand before lowering the cake all the way down to the platter with the icing spatula. Then carefully remove the icing spatula and smooth out the small area where the icing meets the platter if necessary.

Hold the knife perpendicular to the chocolate chunk. Stabilize the chunk with your thumb or against your torso if you have a big enough piece of chocolate. The piece in the photograph is smaller than recommended for making shavings. Because white chocolate is softer than dark chocolate it is possible to get shavings from a smaller chunk.

Making White or Chocolate Shavings

The simplest way to make chocolate shavings is to purchase a large block of white or dark chocolate (see information on ingredients), at least one or two pounds. Place the chocolate block smooth side up on a cutting board. Be sure you are wearing an apron or your "baking" clothes because this gets a little messy. Hold your French (chef's) knife perpendicular to the surface of the chocolate, with the blade against the chocolate's surface. Press down on the blade and, at the same time, draw the blade toward you. This usually causes the chocolate block to come forward and you will likely need to use your torso to keep it securely on the counter. The shavings will accumulate at the edge of the knife. After a few scrapes, use the knife to set the shavings off to the side and continue this until you have plenty of shavings. You will want to turn the chocolate block 90 degrees after every few sets of strokes.

Getting Crazy in Your Kitchen

So, I was once a professional chef and I went to culinary school, blah, blah, blah! Yes, very good to know. What I want you to realize is that everything photographed in this book was made in my own kitchen, using my oven, which is at least 20, probably closer to 30, years old, my trusty Kitchen Aid mixer which is also 20 years old, and basic items you can easily pick up at common stores that carry kitchen equipment. I found my trifle bowl at a discount store and they were selling it as a salad bowl for less than $10. Sometimes things don't always go perfectly, that is why you cover the cake in nuts, or maybe if the whole thing gets way from you just run to the store for a quart of heavy whipping cream and some fresh fruit and turn the whole thing into a trifle. People will love it. We have another saying in the food industry – "No one will ever know" – this is not to say that you should not take care when working on your project, but if you have a failure do not give up.

I hope you will try out new combinations. If you read the introduction then you will remember that my final exam for my students in pastry class was to take elements from different recipes and combine them to make something new. The Lemon Meringues I mentioned were just one example. The possibilities are endless. This cake with that filling, combine nut meringue layers like Marjolaine layers or Dacquoise layers with other fillings and icings or even other cake layers too. The trifle combinations are completely endless. I have even put ganache or chocolate mousse between two cookies (my favorite cookies are the Chocolate Chip Oatmeal Cookies but the Chocolate Chocolate Chunk Cookies are also very good for this). Think outside the box, come up with new stuff. This is where the magic happens, right in your own kitchen. Get in there and Get Crazy!

Cakes, Tortes & Cheesecakes

Baking Pure & Simple

Cakes, Tortes & Cheesecakes

Pumpkin Cheesecake [page 50]

Banana Cake

¾ cup vegetable shortening
2 cups sugar
3 eggs
1 teaspoon vanilla
2¾ cups cake flour
1½ teaspoons baking soda
1½ teaspoons baking powder
1¼ teaspoons salt
1¼ cups buttermilk
5 bananas, mashed by hand or in a food processor
¾ cup chopped pecans or walnuts
1 to 1½ cups additional chopped nuts for decorating

1 recipe Cream Cheese Icing (right)

Preheat oven to 350°F. Cream shortening and sugar together. Slowly add eggs one at a time, scraping down the bowl after each addition. Add vanilla. Sift dry ingredients together. Add to mixture alternately with buttermilk, mixing just until combined. Add mashed bananas and ¾ cup chopped nuts. Bake in 2 greased and floured 10 by 2-inch round cake pans for 40 to 50 minutes or until a wooden pick inserted in the center comes out clean. Cool completely. See instructions on Removing Cakes from Pans on page 11.

Cream Cheese Icing

1 cup unsalted butter, room temperature
1½ pounds cream cheese, chilled
1¾ cups powdered sugar
½ tablespoon vanilla

Cream butter until smooth. Add cream cheese one half pound at a time, scraping down the bowl after each addition and continue creaming until the mixture has a uniform consistency. Add powdered sugar gradually and mix. Add vanilla and mix until smooth. Makes enough filling and icing for a 2-layer Banana or Carrot Cake.

Refer to the section on Assembling and Icing Cakes on page 11, filling and icing the layers with Cream Cheese Icing and pressing the remaining chopped nuts into the sides and over the top of the cake. Serves 16.

Gluten-Free Maple Banana Cake: Substitute 2 cups maple syrup for the 2 cups sugar and 3 cups Gluten-Free Baking Mix (page 8) for the 2¾ cups cake flour, omit buttermilk, and increase chopped pecans in batter to 1½ cups.

9x13 45min

Carrot Cake

1⅔ pound carrots, finely shredded
2¼ cups sugar
1½ cups vegetable oil
4 eggs
1¾ cups flour
1 teaspoon salt
2 teaspoons baking soda
1 teaspoon cinnamon
½ teaspoon nutmeg
½ teaspoon allspice
1 cup golden raisins
⅔ cup chopped walnuts
1 to 1½ cups additional chopped walnuts for decoration

1 recipe Cream Cheese Icing (page 19)

Preheat oven to 350°F. Place shredded carrots into a very large mixing bowl and set aside. Combine sugar and oil in an electric mixing bowl and mix with the paddle attachment on low speed until combined. Add eggs one at a time, mixing and scraping down the sides of the bowl after each addition. Sift dry ingredients. Add dry ingredients slowly. Scrape the bowl down once and add raisins and nuts. Mix just until blended. Pour the mixture over the carrots and gently stir together with a sturdy wooden spoon.

Pour batter into 2 greased and floured 10 by 2-inch round cake pans or a greased 13 by 9-inch baking pan and bake until a wooden pick inserted in the center comes out clean, about 45 to 50 minutes. Allow to cool completely in the pans on racks. See instructions on removing cakes from pans on page 11. Fill and ice with Cream Cheese Icing using instructions on Assembling and Icing Cakes on page 11, pressing additional chopped walnuts against the sides and sprinkling them on the top to decorate. Serves 16.

German Chocolate Cake

3/8 cup water
3 ounces semi-sweet chocolate, chopped
½ cup unsalted butter
¼ cup shortening
1½ cups sugar
3 eggs
¾ teaspoon vanilla
1¾ cups flour
1½ teaspoon baking soda
½ teaspoon salt
¾ cup buttermilk

1 recipe German Chocolate Icing (right)

Preheat oven to 350°F. In a small saucepan, boil water. Remove pan from heat. Add chocolate and stir until melted, set aside. In a mixing bowl, cream butter, shortening and sugar. Slowly add eggs to the creamed mixture, occasionally scraping down the sides of the bowl between additions. Blend in the melted chocolate and vanilla. Sift dry ingredients. Add dry ingredients alternately with buttermilk, mixing just until combined.

Pour batter into two greased and floured 10 by 2-inch cake pans or a greased 13 by 9-inch baking pan and bake for 20 to 25 minutes or until a wooden pick inserted in the center comes out clean. Remove cakes from cake pans when completely cooled. See instructions on Removing Cakes from Pans on page 11. Fill and ice with German Chocolate Icing (see instructions on Assembling and Icing Cakes on page 11.) Serves 16.

German Chocolate Icing

12 ounces evaporated milk
1¾ cups sugar
5 eggs, beaten
5⅓ ounces unsalted butter
1 teaspoon vanilla
2 cups sweetened flaked coconut
4 cups chopped pecans

Combine evaporated milk, sugar, eggs, butter and vanilla in the top of a double boiler or a metal bowl over simmering water in a saucepan. Whisk often while cooking until thickened, about 10 to 15 minutes. Add coconut and pecans. Cool completely, first on the counter for about 30 minutes, then stir once or twice before refrigerating. Do not cover until cooled. Makes more than enough filling and icing for a German Chocolate Cake.

Chocolate Chocolate Chip Zucchini Cake

½ cup unsalted butter
1¼ cups honey
½ cup vegetable oil
3 eggs
½ cup buttermilk
¾ cup tapioca flour*
1 cup ground flaxseed or flaxseed meal*
¾ cup rice flour*
¾ cup coconut flour*
½ teaspoon allspice
½ teaspoon cinnamon
½ teaspoon salt
2 teaspoons baking soda
¼ cup cocoa
3 cups zucchini, grated
2 cups semi-sweet chocolate chips or chunks
1 cup raisins
1 cup chopped walnuts or pecans

1 recipe Sour Cream Chocolate Icing (right)

Preheat oven to 325°F. Melt butter in a medium pan. Remove from heat. Whisk in honey, oil, buttermilk and eggs. Stir dry ingredients, tapioca flour through cocoa, together into a large bowl. Add the buttermilk mixture. Stir in zucchini, chocolate chips, raisins and nuts. Bake in a greased 13 by 9-inch baking pan or two round greased 10 by 2-inch pans for 40 to 50 minutes or until a wooden pick inserted in the center comes out clean. Cool completely. See instructions for Removing Cakes from Pans on page 11.

Fill and ice with Sour Cream Chocolate icing (see Assembling and Icing Cakes on page 11.) Finish the sides with a cake comb and then pipe alternating half rosettes from a pastry bag or plastic bag through a star tip. Find out more on pastry bags and tips in the Equipment section (pages 9-10). Decorate with fresh pansies, if desired. For an alternate presentation, cover the cake with chocolate shavings. Serves 16.

Wheat version: To make this cake with wheat flour, substitute all the flours and the flaxseed for a total of 3¼ cups flour and bake at 350°F for 40 to 45 minutes.

Oat Bran Version: *Reduce all 4 above ingredients by ¼ cup each and add 1 cup oat bran if desired.

Sour Cream Chocolate Icing

1½ pounds semi-sweet chocolate
1½ pounds sour cream

Melt chocolate in the top of a double boiler or in a large metal bowl over simmering water in a saucepan. Remove the bowl from the top of the pan and place on a towel or cutting board. Whisk in sour cream by hand. Use immediately. If the icing becomes too solid to work with return the bowl to the top of the pan of simmering water and stir gently until softened, then whisk together again. Makes enough to ice and fill one cake.

The flavor combination of lemon and coconut is a classic. This cake is light, sweet and tart. Perfect for summertime.

Lemon Coconut Torte

1 Yellow Chiffon Cake prepared with lemon zest, (below),
split into thirds horizontally (see Splitting Cakes Horizontally on page 11)
1 recipe Lemon Curd (page 28)
1 recipe Swiss Meringue Buttercream (page 28)
1¼ cups unsweetened small flake coconut
½ recipe Simple Syrup (page 103)

1 cup coconut shavings or additional flake coconut for decorating.

Combine the 1¼ cups small flake coconut with the Swiss Meringue Buttercream.

Place the first cake layer, cut side up, on a cake round or a serving platter. Brush the cake gently until just moistened with approximately one-third of the Simple Syrup. Spread ⅓-inch layer of the coconut buttercream mixture on the cake layer. Top with another layer of cake, cut side up, and brush with another third of the simple syrup. Top with ⅓-inch layer of lemon curd. Add the final layer of chiffon cake, cut side up, and brush with the remaining simple syrup. Ice the cake according to the directions for Assembling and Icing Cakes on page 11 with the remaining coconut buttercream and decorate with 16 piped rosettes from a pastry or plastic bag, fitted with a star tip, evenly spaced around the edge on the top. See the Equipment section (pages 9-10) for more on pastry bags and tips. Gently press the coconut shavings or flakes on the sides of the cake and sprinkle them on top. Serves 16.

Yellow Chiffon Cake

1⅓ cups cake flour or 1½ cups spelt flour
¾ cup sugar
1½ teaspoons baking powder
¼ teaspoon salt
4 egg yolks
⅓ cup water
¼ cup vegetable oil
1 teaspoon vanilla
1 teaspoon lemon zest or orange zest
4 egg whites

Preheat oven to 350°F. Sift flour, sugar, baking powder and salt together in a large bowl. Make a well in the center. Combine egg yolks, water, oil, vanilla and zest in the well and whisk together, then combine with the dry ingredients, mixing until smooth. Whip whites separately with an electric mixer until stiff. Fold the whites into the batter in thirds. Bake in a 10 by 2-inch round cake pan (do not grease the pan) for approximately 20 - 25 minutes or until a wooden pick inserted in the center comes out clean. Allow to cool completely. See instructions for Removing Cakes from Pans on page 11.

Note: If making only half a recipe as for either of the Dacquoise cakes later in this chapter, spread the batter very thin and evenly in a 13 by 9-inch pan lined with parchment paper and bake only15 to 18 minutes.

Lemon Curd

8 egg yolks
½ cup lemon juice (juice of 3 to 4 small lemons)
1½ teaspoons lemon zest (zest of approximately 1 small lemon)
⅔ cup sugar
¼ cup unsalted butter

Whisk together egg yolks, juice, zest and sugar in the top of a double boiler or in a metal bowl over gently simmering water. Cook until thick, whisking frequently for about 10 to 15 minutes. Add butter and stir until completely melted. Remove from the top of the simmering water to cool. Place in a glass container for storage. Cool uncovered in the refrigerator until chilled, then cover. Keep refrigerated until used. Makes 2 cups.

Swiss Meringue Buttercream

1 cup egg whites (approximately 7)
1½ cups sugar
2 cups unsalted butter, almost room temperature
1 teaspoon vanilla

Combine egg whites and sugar in a metal bowl over a pan of gently simmering water. Heat the mixture, whisking almost constantly for about 8 to 10 minutes until the sugar is dissolved and the mixture is no longer grainy. Take care that the egg whites do not cook on the side of the bowl by whisking almost continuously.

Place the mixture in the bowl of an electric mixer. Whip on medium for a few minutes until frothy and then increase speed to high and continue to whip triple in volume and shiny peaks form, about 5 to 10 minutes. Reduce the speed of the mixer to low and slowly add softened butter in chunks. The mixture will separate and then come back together again once all the butter is added. Add the vanilla.

If it is a warm day the mixture may look soupy rather than fluffy. Try holding a bag of frozen vegetables against the side of the bowl while whipping at a slightly reduced speed. The mixture should become fluffy in a few minutes. This buttercream is best if used immediately. To store, cover in the refrigerator or freeze in an airtight container. Allow the buttercream to return to room temperature and whip with an electric mixer to restore consistency before using. If the icing separates, whip it again with the electric mixer until it is smooth. Makes approximately 3 cups.

Irish Stout Cake

4 ounces unsweetened chocolate
½ cup unsalted butter
1½ cups brown sugar
½ cup molasses
2 eggs
2 teaspoons vanilla
1 cup stout beer
2 cups flour
½ teaspoon salt
2 teaspoons baking soda
½ cup buttermilk

Cream Cheese Icing (page 19) or Sour Cream Chocolate Icing (page 25)
⅓ cup Irish cream whiskey, such as Bailey's

chocolate shavings (optional)

Preheat oven to 350°F. Melt the chocolate in the top of a double boiler or a metal bowl over simmering water in a saucepan, set aside.

Cream butter and brown sugar. Add one egg at a time, mixing until thoroughly incorporated and scraping down the sides of the bowl after each addition. Add molasses and vanilla and mix until combined, scraping down the bowl. Add a little of the batter to the melted chocolate and stir to combine completely. Add the chocolate mixture back to the batter and mix until combined.

Slowly add the beer to the batter in intervals, scraping down the sides of the bowl between additions. Sift the flour, salt and baking soda. When the beer has been fully incorporated, add half of the flour mixture to the batter and mix until thoroughly combined. Add the buttermilk, again scraping down the sides of the bowl and mixing until fully incorporated. Add the remaining flour mixture and mix thoroughly. Pour the batter into a greased 10-inch round spring form pan. Bake for 45 to 50 minutes or until a wooden pick comes out clean when inserted in the center.

Allow the cake to cool completely. Run a knife around the edge of the cake before removing the outer ring of the spring form pan. Refer to the directions for Splitting Cake Layers Horizontally on page 11 to slice the cake into two even layers.

Prepare the desired icing and slowly mix in the Irish cream whiskey. Ice and fill the cake per the directions for Assembling and Icing Cakes on page 11. Decorate with chocolate shavings, if desired. Serves 16.

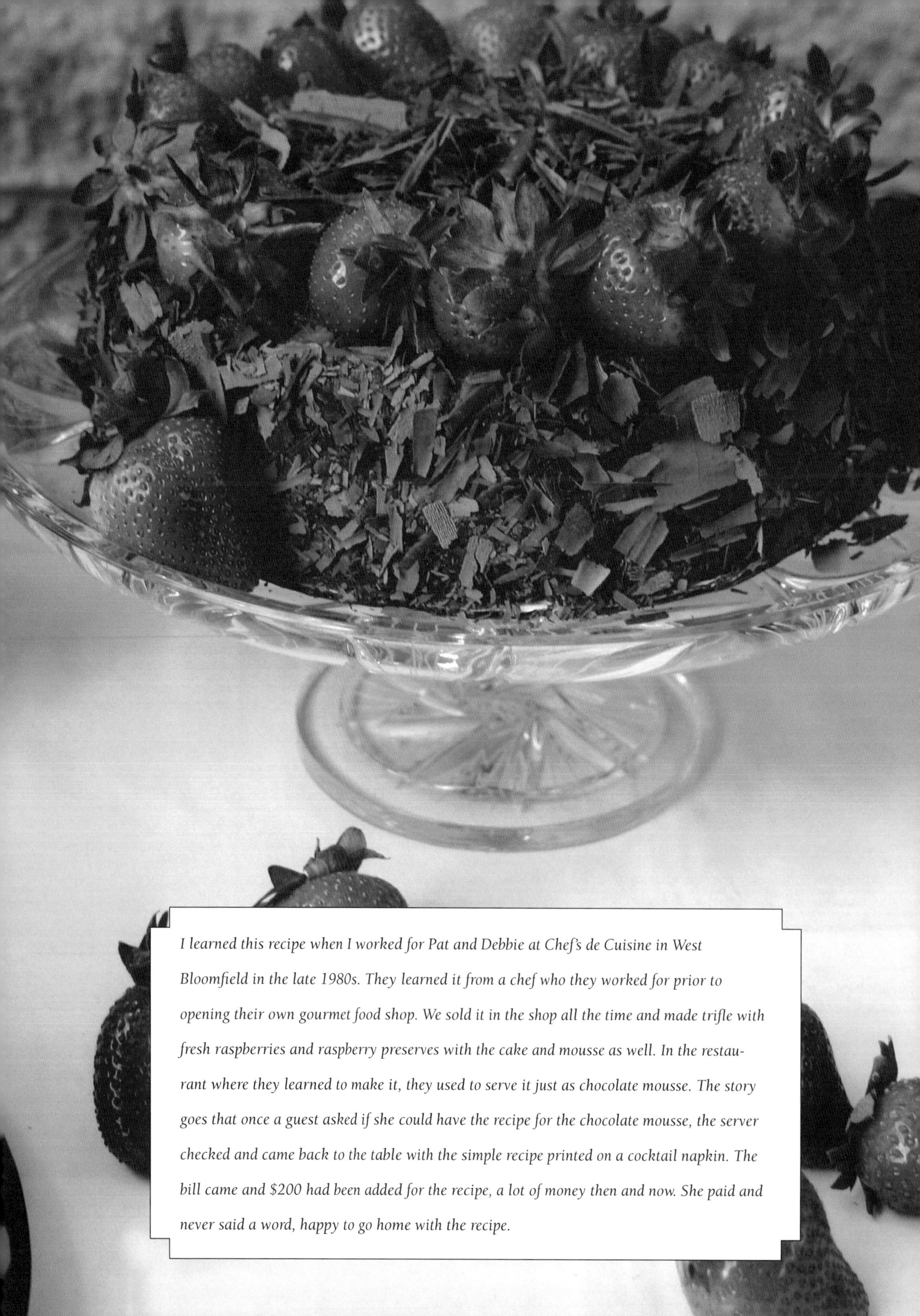

I learned this recipe when I worked for Pat and Debbie at Chef's de Cuisine in West Bloomfield in the late 1980s. They learned it from a chef who they worked for prior to opening their own gourmet food shop. We sold it in the shop all the time and made trifle with fresh raspberries and raspberry preserves with the cake and mousse as well. In the restaurant where they learned to make it, they used to serve it just as chocolate mousse. The story goes that once a guest asked if she could have the recipe for the chocolate mousse, the server checked and came back to the table with the simple recipe printed on a cocktail napkin. The bill came and $200 had been added for the recipe, a lot of money then and now. She paid and never said a word, happy to go home with the recipe.

Flourless Chocolate Cake with Strawberries

Warning: *This cake contains raw eggs. The cake batter doubles as the chocolate mousse filling. Consumption of raw eggs may increase your risk of food borne illness. With proper handling this should not be an issue for most people. Some people may not wish to consume raw eggs and should use the alternate preparation at the end of the recipe, substituting the Soft Chocolate Ganache for the chocolate mousse. Make the ganache several hours before you plan to put the cake together so it will have time to set up.*

1 pound semi-sweet chocolate
2 cups unsalted butter
16 egg whites
16 egg yolks
2 tablespoons sugar
2 tablespoon coffee liqueur or 1 tablespoon vanilla
2 tablespoons strawberry jam (optional)
¼ recipe Simple Syrup (page 103)
1 tablespoon coffee liqueur and 1 tablespoon cognac
2 to 3 cups chocolate shavings - shaved from a 1-2 pound block of semi-sweet chocolate
12 medium or 16 small fresh, perfect strawberries with hulls, rinsed and dried

Preheat oven to 350°F. Melt the chocolate and butter in a large metal bowl over a pan with simmering water. Remove from the top of the pan and allow to cool slightly. Meanwhile, whip the yolks with an electric mixer for about 5 minutes or until they are tripled in volume and light in color. Whisk the yolks and the liqueur or vanilla into the melted chocolate mixture by hand. Using a clean bowl and whisk, whip the whites with an electric mixer, adding sugar when they begin to look frothy. Continue to whip until peaks form. Fold the whites into the chocolate mixture in three stages. Divide the mixture in half, placing one half in a glass storage container and refrigerating; this is the chocolate mousse filling. Divide the rest of the mixture into two greased, round 10 by 2-inch cake pans. Bake for 20 to 25 minutes or until a wooden pick inserted in the cake comes out clean and the surface of the cake springs back if touched lightly. The layers will rise very high at first. As they cool they will fall back in the center, pull away from the sides and possibly crack. Allow to cool completely.

The chocolate mousse filling will need to be refrigerated for several hours or overnight in order to be fully set up. Refrigerate the cakes once cooled until the mousse is ready. See instructions for Removing Cakes from Pans on page 11. Place both the layers on cake cardboards, inverting after removing from pans so that the top sides are up.

Brush the bottom cake layer with Simple Syrup mixed with the coffee liqueur and then spread with a little strawberry jam (optional). Top with a layer of the chilled mousse, bringing the mousse up and just over the level of the raised edges of the cake sides or to about ⅓-inch thickness. Top with the other layer, this time upside down, and brush with the simple syrup. Next, top and ice the cake with the remaining mousse. If you are not planning to serve the cake immediately, wrap it in plastic wrap and chill until about an hour before serving.

Continued on page 33

Continued from page 31

Flourless Chocolate Cake with Strawberries

To finish the torte, place a strawberry on a slight angle on top of the cake about half an inch from the edge with the hull toward the outside. Place another strawberry opposite the first on the other side of the cake for proper spacing, as if at 12 and 6 on the face of a clock. Now place two more at 90° angles to the first two (at 3 and 9 on the clock) and then place two or three strawberries along the perimeter of the cake in each quarter, so that each piece will have its own whole strawberry. Cover the cake with chocolate shavings by pressing them gently into the sides and piling them up on the top. Serve immediately or refrigerate until serving. Slice the cake so that everyone gets a piece with a whole strawberry. Refrigerate leftovers promptly. Serves 12 to 16.

Alternate preparation with Ganache instead of Chocolate Mousse: Prepare only half a recipe of the flourless chocolate cake mixture and bake the entire amount in the two round greased 10 by 2-inch pans. Substitute Soft Chocolate Ganache (recipe below) for the chocolate mousse. Finish preparing completely prior to chilling the cake; the chocolate shavings will not stick to the ganache if it is too cold. Chill the cake until 3 to 4 hours prior to serving. If it is a very hot day, then chill until about 1 hour before serving. The cake prepared with the ganache is best if it is allowed to come to room temperature before serving.

Chocolate Ganache

1 pound 2 ounces semi-sweet chocolate, chopped
2 cups heavy cream
2 tablespoons coffee liqueur or other liqueur (optional)

Place cream in a heavy bottom saucepan and bring to a boil. Remove from heat immediately. Add chocolate. Whisk until smooth. Add liqueur and mix. Allow to cool completely but do not refrigerate; this will take several hours. On hot days or if it does not set up to a firm enough consistency in several hours refrigerate, but check it every 20 minutes or so to make sure it is not becoming too firm to work with. Ganache will be very firm when chilled, so if it gets too firm just leave it on the counter and allow it to return to room temperature before using it to fill the cake. Store leftover ganache in the refrigerator. Makes 4 cups.

Soft Chocolate Ganache: Use 14 ounces semi-sweet chocolate instead of 1 pound 2 ounces.

Sweet Soft Chocolate Ganache Glaze: Follow recipe for Soft Chocolate Ganache; cool slightly but do not allow to set up. Stir in ¼ cup light corn syrup.

This cake is the first of several variations which can be made with the Flourless Chocolate Cake recipe. It combines the flavors of dark chocolate and crystallized ginger for a decadently rich cake. The inspiration for this torte was a chocolate ginger truffle.

Dark Chocolate Ginger Torte

Also pictured on page 7

2 layers Flourless Chocolate Cake
(page 31; prepare half the recipe and bake all the batter in two greased round 10 by 2-inch cake pans)

1 recipe Soft Chocolate Ganache
(page 33, fully set and at room temperature; omit the liqueur)

¼ cup crystallized ginger, minced
¼ recipe Simple Syrup (page 103)
12 to 16 slivers of crystallized ginger
2 to 3 cups chocolate shavings, shaved from a 1-2 pound block of semi-sweet chocolate
(see Making Chocolate Shavings on page 12)

Place one layer of the cake on a cake cardboard or serving platter, right side up. Brush the cake with about half of the Simple Syrup. Spread about ¼ of the Soft Chocolate Ganache over the layer of cake. Top with the minced crystallized ginger evenly distributing it and pressing it gently into the ganache. Top with the other layer of cake, upside down, and brush with the remaining Simple Syrup. Top and ice with the chocolate ganache.

Fill a pastry bag or plastic bag fitted with a star tip with the remaining chocolate ganache and pipe rosettes all around the edge of the cake. See the Equipment section (pages 9-10) for more on pastry bags and tips. Top each rosette with a sliver of crystallized ginger. Gently press the chocolate shavings into the sides of the cake. Top the cake with more chocolate shavings all the way to the edge of the rosettes. Chill for several hours. Remove from the refrigerator about 3 to 4 hours prior to serving. This cake is best if allowed to return to room temperature prior to serving. Serves 12 to 16.

This is another variation of torte using the flourless chocolate cake. Each of these variations is naturally gluten-free since the cake and fillings contain no flour. We came up with this one when I worked in the hotel. Cappuccino became popular in the 1980s, so we created a torte to simulate its flavors.

Cappuccino Torte

2 layers Flourless Chocolate Cake
(page 31, prepare half the recipe and bake all the batter in 2 greased round 10 by 2-inch cake pans)

½ recipe Chocolate Ganache
(page 33, prepared with 3 tablespoons coffee liqueur, chilled but allowed to return to room temperature)

2 cups heavy whipping cream
½ teaspoon cinnamon
1 teaspoon vanilla
½ cup powdered sugar
¼ cup Simple Syrup (page 103)
2 to 3 cups chocolate shavings - shaved from a 1-2 pound block of semi-sweet chocolate

Place one layer of the cake on a cake cardboard or serving platter, right side up. Brush with about half of the simple syrup. Spread the chocolate ganache over the layer of cake. Top with the second layer of cake, upside down. Using your spatula clean the edges of the cake so that the ganache is flush with the sides of the cake layers. Whip the heavy cream together with the cinnamon, vanilla and powdered sugar until the consistency is firm enough for icing a cake. Ice the cake with the whipped cream, refer to the section on Icing Cakes on page 11.

Fill a pastry bag or plastic bag fitted with a star tip with whipped cream and pipe rosettes all around the edge of the cake. See the Equipment section (pages 9-10) for information on pastry bags and tips. Gently press the chocolate shavings into the sides of the cake. Top the cake with more chocolate shavings all the way to the edge of the rosettes. Chill for a few hours before serving, but remove the cake from refrigerator to a cool place 1 to 2 hours before serving. Serves 12 to 16.

I learned about Dacquoise and other meringue layers when I worked in the hotel. So many recipes call for egg yolks that we would always end up with large quantities of egg whites. We used them in Swiss Meringue Buttercream, but still we had more egg whites leftover. Because ground nuts comprise the structure of the layers, Dacquoise and Marjolaine recipes call for very small amounts of flour. Substituting tapioca or rice flour for wheat flour will make these layers gluten-free.

Cherry Chocolate Dacquoise

1 recipe Dacquoise (page 40)
½ recipe Yellow Chiffon Cake (page 27, baked in a 13 x 9-inch pan, lined with parchment paper on the bottom)
½ cup Simple Syrup (page 103)
½ recipe Chocolate Ganache (page 33, fully cooled, but not chilled)
1 recipe Custard Buttercream (page 41)
1 cup cherry preserves, chopped
2 cups sliced almonds, lightly toasted

Slice the layer of Dacquoise lengthwise into two halves, each 13 by 4½-inches. Lift off of the baking pan and carefully remove the parchment paper on which the Dacquoise was baked. Place one layer of Dacquoise on the serving platter for the torte. Gently slip clean pieces of parchment paper under each edge of the Dacquoise layer so that the parchment is only about ½-inch underneath, but extends out to cover the visible area of the platter. Spread a ¼-inch layer of Chocolate Ganache over the Dacquoise. Place the second layer of Dacquoise over the ganache. Refrigerate these layers while you prepare the cherry Custard Buttercream.

Reserve 2 tablespoons of the chopped cherry preserves for garnish. Combine the remaining chopped cherry preserves with the Custard Buttercream. Spread a layer of cherry Custard Buttercream over the top layer of Dacquoise. Slice the Yellow Chiffon Cake lengthwise into two 13 by 4½-inch layers. Gently remove the baking parchment from the chiffon layer and place the cake upside down on top of the cherry Custard Buttercream layer. Using a pastry brush, moisten the chiffon layer with Simple Syrup, you will have about half of the Simple Syrup and one 13 by 4½-inch layer of chiffon cake leftover. Refrigerate the torte for about 30 minutes. Using the remaining cherry custard buttercream ice the top of the torte and then the sides. See page 11 for details on Icing Cakes.

To decorate the top, partially fill a pastry or plastic bag fitted with a ¼-inch diameter round tip with the cherry Custard Buttercream. See the Equipment section (pages 9-10) for information on pastry bags and tips. Beginning at the short edge of the torte about an inch from the corner, make a zigzag line the length of the torte. Move over about ¼-inch and make another zigzag line that follows the form of the first line. Next make small circles all in a straight line the length of the torte, estimating one circle on each slice of torte. The circles should be about the size of a nickel and have about ¼-inch between each one. Using a very small spoon or another pastry or plastic bag with the same ¼-inch diameter round tip, place a small dot of the reserved cherry preserves in the center of each buttercream circle.

Continued on page 40

Continued from page 39

Cherry Chocolate Dacquoise

Refrigerate the torte for at least 2 hours before slicing and then it leave out at room temperature for about an hour before gently pressing the almond slices onto the sides. After the almonds are on, carefully remove the parchment from beneath the edges of the torte. This should allow you to have a nice clean serving platter and finished edge appearance for the torte. If you do have any stray areas of buttercream on the serving platter, clean them up with a little moistened towel just before serving. This torte is best if removed from the refrigerator for about an hour prior to serving. Serves 10 to 12.

Dacquoise Layers

2 egg whites
½ cup sugar
1 cup ground almonds or almond flour
3 tablespoons flour or spelt flour

Preheat oven to 450°F. Heat sugar and egg whites in a mixing bowl over simmering water until the sugar is dissolved. Remove from heat and whip mixture with an electric mixer on medium for a few minutes or until frothy and then increase speed to high until soft stiff peaks form. Combine the almonds and the flour. Fold the nut mixture into the whites. Spread the mixture on a greased piece of 13 by 9-inch parchment paper lining the same size pan. Grease the corners of the pan then line the sheet pan with the parchment paper and grease the parchment paper. Greasing the corners of the pan first will help the parchment stick to the pan. Spread the mixture into the pan evenly using a handheld spatula or a bench scraper. Wet your fingers with cold water if you need to use them to spread the mixture in certain areas. It will be only about a ¼-inch thick. Bake at 450°F for the first 7 minutes, then turn the heat down to 350°F for another 4 to 5 minutes until lightly browned. Remove from the oven and allow to cool completely. Makes one 13 by 9-inch layer. Once cooled, slice lengthwise into two 13 by 4½-inch layers.

Custard Buttercream

¼ recipe Custard (page 103), slightly cooled
1 pound unsalted butter, chilled slightly

Custard Buttercream is really just custard with butter whipped into it. Generally, something is added to it for more flavor and sweetness. It has a rich creamy flavor on its own.

Prepare ¼ recipe Custard and allow it to cool for about 10 minutes. Transfer the custard into the bowl of an electric mixer and attach the whip. Whip the custard for a few minutes, allowing the steam to be released. Cut the butter into tablespoon size chunks and add to the custard while whipping at medium speed. Continue to add the butter until it is all incorporated, then increase the speed of the mixer to high for a few minutes. The buttercream should be shiny and thick and it should ripple as it mixes like fully whipped cream. It should be slightly pale in color and have air bubbles once you lift out the whip.

If the buttercream seems too thick and does not have this whipped consistency, you can try two things. One is to refrigerate the mixture for about 15 minutes, then continue to whip it. Repeat this several times, each time removing it from the refrigerator after just 15 minutes and whipping it again, always scraping down the sides before returning it to the mixer. You can also try holding any kind of cold pack or a sealed bag of frozen vegetables or ice cubes on the outside of the bowl while whipping. This works very well and should only take about 5 minutes to return the mixture to the right consistency. Makes approximately 3 cups.

This is probably the most challenging recipe in the book. The tricky part is getting the ganache to just the right consistency to spread as icing. Remember you can always use a few more sliced almonds and cover the whole torte, instead of just the sides. If you are feeling powerful, this is a great torte to try. It is like Boston Cream Pie, with a crunch!

Chocolate Custard Dacquoise

1 recipe Dacquoise layers (page 40)
½ recipe Yellow Chiffon Cake with prepared with orange rind
(page 27, follow instructions for baking on parchment paper in a 13 by 9-inch pan)

¼ cup Simple Syrup (page 103)
1 recipe Chocolate Ganache, (page 33, fully cooled, but not chilled)
½ recipe Custard, (page 103, completely chilled)
1 to 1½ cups sliced almonds, lightly toasted

Slice the layer of Dacquoise lengthwise into two halves, each 13 by 4½-inches. Lift off of the baking pan and carefully remove the parchment paper on which the Dacquoise was baked. Place one layer of Dacquoise on the serving platter for the torte. Gently slip clean pieces of parchment paper under each edge of the Dacquoise layer so that the parchment is only about ½-inch underneath, but extends out to cover the visible area of the platter. Spread a ¼-inch layer of Chocolate Ganache over the Dacquoise. Place the second layer of Dacquoise over the ganache. Refrigerate the layers for about 30 minutes.

Next spread a layer of Custard over the second layer of Dacquoise. Slice the Yellow Chiffon Cake layer lengthwise into two 13 by 4½-inch layers. Gently remove the parchment paper from one layer of the cake and place the cake upside down on top of the custard layer. Using a pastry brush, moisten the chiffon layer with Simple Syrup, you will have some custard and one 13 by 4½-inch layer of chiffon cake leftover.

Using the remaining Ganache ice the sides of the torte and then the top. This is contrary to the instructions on page 11 on Icing Cakes. Icing the sides of this torte first adds stability to the soft custard layer. Once the top has been iced, run the spatula along the sides again and then trim off the excess ganache moving the spatula toward the center horizontally along the top of the torte. Press the sliced almonds on the sides and, if you wish, sprinkle them over the top as well. Gently remove the parchment paper and push any of the almonds back into place. Refrigerate the torte completely for at least 2 hours. Remove it from the refrigerator one to two hours prior to serving. Serves 10 to 12.

Note: Make individual trifles with the leftover Custard and Yellow Chiffon Cake. Just whip some heavy cream with a little powdered sugar and vanilla and layer along with Custard, Yellow Chiffon Cake with fresh fruit in Margarita glasses. See the Fresh Berry Trifle recipe on page 104 for details.

Marjolaine

1 recipe Marjolaine Layers (page 45)
1 recipe Ganache (page 33)
½ recipe Swiss Meringue Buttercream (page 28)
3 tablespoons hazelnut liqueur
½ cup chopped, toasted almonds
¼ cup chopped, toasted hazelnuts

Prepare ganache a day ahead of time and allow it to set up in a cool place but do not refrigerate.

Prepare Swiss Meringue Buttercream and add the hazelnut liqueur. Slice cooled Marjolaine layers into 4 equal strips, each approximately 4½ by 13 inches. Carefully remove one strip of the Marjolaine from the parchment paper and place it on the surface you will use to construct the torte. This could be a long narrow cutting board or a sheet pan. Top with a layer of buttercream, then add another strip of Marjolaine. Top with a layer of ganache then refrigerate for 15 to 30 minutes, especially if the ganache is soft. Once the ganache is firm add the next strip of Marjolaine and top with another layer of buttercream. Top with the remaining strip of Marjolaine and then refrigerate for another 30 minutes. Ice the entire torte with a thin layer of buttercream and refrigerate for 15 minutes. This is referred to as a crumb layer and is meant to seal in the edges before the final outer layer of icing is applied. Cover the entire torte in ganache, taking care to square off the edges. Refer to the section on Icing Cakes on page 11. Refrigerate for a few minutes before pressing the almonds onto the sides and sprinkling the hazelnuts across the top. Fully chill for several hours or overnight before transferring to a serving platter.

Once the torte is fully chilled, insert an icing spatula beneath it and run it all around the bottom to loosen the ganache cleanly from the tray. Have a serving platter nearby and gently lift the torte with the icing spatula before sliding your hand beneath it and transferring it onto the serving platter. Reinsert the icing spatula between your hand and the platter and remove your hand, then gently place the torte fully down on the platter with the spatula, removing the spatula slowly. Allow Marjolaine to stand outside of refrigeration for an hour or so before serving. Serves 10 to 12.

Marjolaine Layers

1 cup egg whites (approximately 7)
⅓ cup sugar
1¼ cups ground almonds, lightly toasted
⅓ cup ground hazelnuts
1 tablespoon flour or rice flour
1 cup sugar

Preheat oven to 350°F. Whip whites with the ⅓ cup sugar until stiff. Combine almonds, hazelnuts, flour and remaining sugar, and fold into the whipped whites. Grease the corners of a 13 by 18-inch sheet pan then line the sheet pan with parchment paper and grease the parchment paper. Greasing the corners of the pan first will help the parchment stick to the pan and make it easier to grease. Spread the mixture into the pan evenly using a handheld spatula or a bench scraper. Wet your fingers with cold water if you need to use them to spread the mixture in certain areas. Bake for 20 to 25 minutes. It will begin to brown after 15 and will be uniformly light brown on top when done. Cool completely.

Marjolaine is another type of nut meringue pastry. I almost did not include this recipe because I could not find praline paste, which is what we used to use in the hotel to flavor one layer of the buttercream. We also made it with six layers of Marjolaine instead of just four. For this adaptation I used hazelnut liqueur to flavor all the buttercream and everyone seemed to enjoy it. The rectangular tortes are a little bit tricky to finish because of the corners, but the result is worth it.

Orange Bundt Cake with Chocolate Glaze

1 cup unsalted butter
1 cup sugar
3 egg yolks
1½ teaspoons orange liqueur
2 cups flour
1½ teaspoons baking powder
1½ teaspoons baking soda
1¼ cups sour cream
1½ tablespoons orange zest
1 cup chopped pecans
3 egg whites

½ cup orange juice
¼ cup sugar
¼ cup orange liqueur

Sweet Soft Chocolate Ganache Glaze (page 33)

Preheat oven to 350°F. Cream butter and sugar. Add yolks and the 1½ teaspoons orange liqueur. Sift flour, baking powder and soda. Add dry ingredients to the creamed mixture alternately with sour cream, scraping down the sides of the bowl between additions. Stir in orange zest and pecans. Whip whites until stiff. Fold whites into the batter. Place in greased non-stick bundt pan. Bake for 35 to 40 minutes until a wooden pick inserted in the center of the cake comes out clean. Allow to cool for 10 minutes. Do not remove from the pan.

Combine the orange juice, sugar and ¼ cup of the orange liqueur. Poke about 15 holes with a wooden pick in the cake. While the cake is still in the pan, pour the orange juice mixture over the cake in stages, allowing it to be absorbed before adding more. Allow the cake to cool for at least an hour. Prepare a cardboard cake round by trimming the edges to a half inch smaller than the outer diameter of the bundt pan and cutting out a circle in the center which is a half an inch wider than the inner circle of the pan's center tube. Loosen the cake around the edges and invert the cake onto the prepared cake round. The cake should fall right out of the bundt pan. Refrigerate to cool completely.

Transfer the cake on the cake cardboard to a cooling rack over a sheet pan and pour fresh, slightly warm (just liquid enough to coat a spoon thickly) Sweet Soft Chocolate Ganache Glaze over the cake, shaking the rack slightly to help the glaze spread out evenly. Leaving the cake on the cardboard, carefully transfer it to a serving plate and chill until ready to serve. Serves 12.

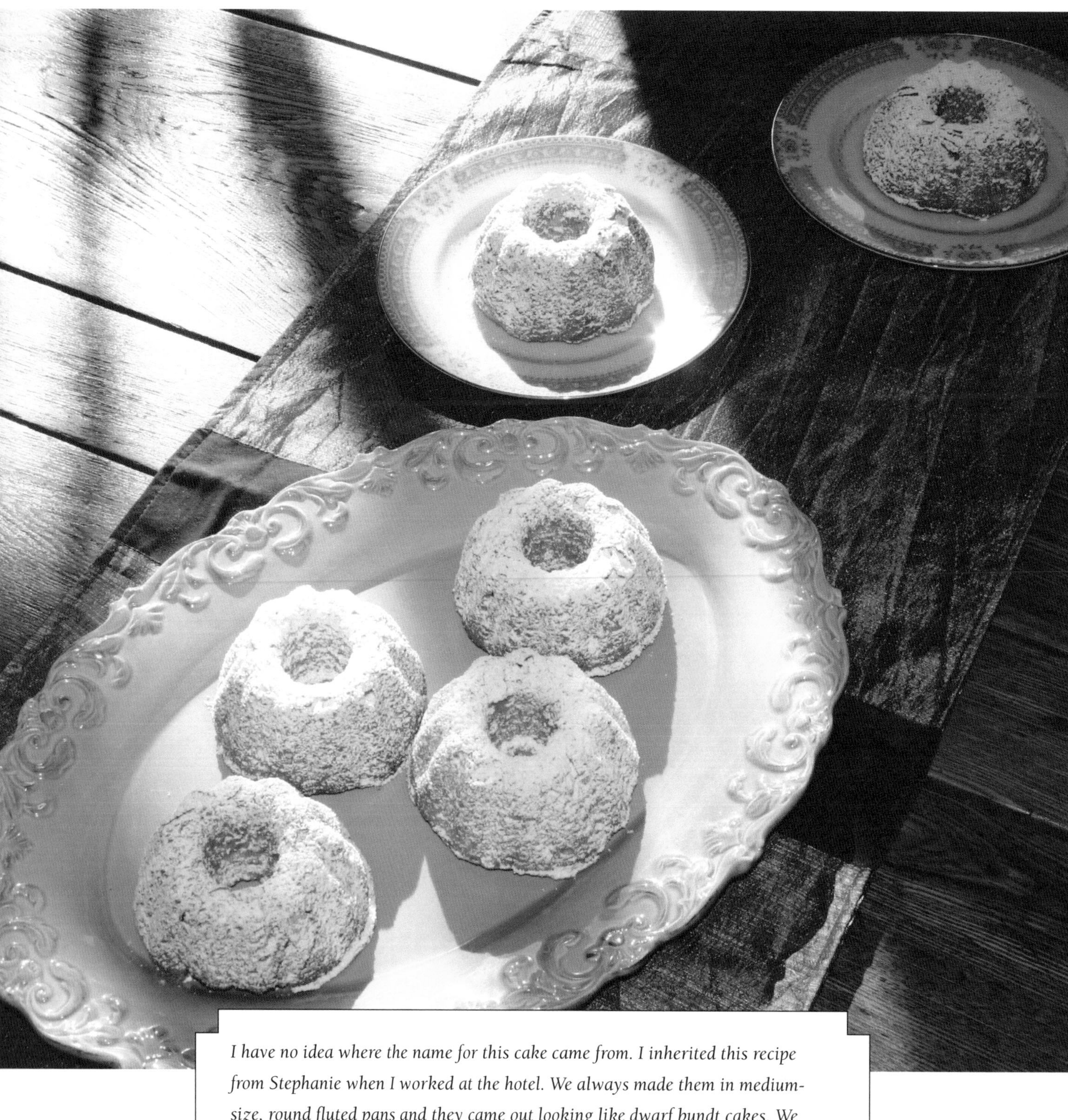

I have no idea where the name for this cake came from. I inherited this recipe from Stephanie when I worked at the hotel. We always made them in medium-size, round fluted pans and they came out looking like dwarf bundt cakes. We filled the centers with cherry filling and each one served about 6 people. I found smaller pans that are about the same shape to make these individual Financiers. The other option is to just make a short bundt cake or to double the recipe for a full size bundt cake.

Financiers

1 cup almond meal
1 cup bread flour
¼ teaspoon salt
¾ teaspoon baking powder
1¼ cups sugar, divided
5 egg whites
1 cup unsalted butter, melted
¼ cup sliced almonds
powdered sugar for dusting

Preheat oven to 400°F. Sift dry ingredients and ¾ cup sugar. Beat whites until frothy and then slowly add the remaining ½ cup sugar. Continue whipping until they form soft peaks. Fold dry ingredients into the whites. Fold melted butter into the batter. Line either 7 greased individual baking molds with center cones or a single bundt pan with the sliced almonds. Scoop the batter into the prepared pan(s).

Bake at 400°F for 5 minutes then decrease the temperature to 375°F, leaving the oven door open for a minute so the heat can escape until the temperature has come down. Continue baking for 15 minutes for individual cakes or until cakes pull away from the sides and spring back when touched lightly. Allow to cool for about 10 minutes before gently loosening with a sharp knife around the center cone and the edges. Remove one by one making sure that all the sides and inner edges are free before gently lifting them out with two hands. Invert on cooling racks and cool completely.

For a single bundt pan bake at 400°F for 5 minutes and then turn heat down to 350°F for another 15 to 20 minutes or until a wooden pick inserted in the center comes out clean. Allow to cool for about 20 minutes before shaking gently to see if it is loose. Once loose, invert onto a cooling rack in one quick motion to remove the cake from the bundt pan. Makes 1 short bunt or 7 individual cakes.

When cakes are completely cooled, dust with powdered sugar through a sifter to finish. Carefully transfer to a serving platter.

Serve Financiers alone or with Chunky Raspberry Sauce (page 53), Lemon Curd (page 28) or vanilla ice cream.

Holiday Financier Bundt: Double the recipe and add ¼ cup each lemon and orange citron, ½ cup chopped dried cherries and ½ cup sliced almonds. Bake at 350°F in a full size bundt pan for 45 to 55 minutes or until a wooden pick inserted in the center comes out clean. When completely cool, dust with powdered sugar.

Pumpkin Cheesecake

Pictured on page 17

½ cup unsalted butter, melted
1½ cups ginger snaps, crushed or ground in a food processor

1½ pounds cream cheese, softened
¾ cup sugar
1 teaspoon cinnamon
1 teaspoon ground ginger
½ teaspoon ground cloves
½ teaspoon ground nutmeg
3 eggs
2 tablespoons brandy
¼ cup maple syrup
¼ cup heavy cream
15 ounces canned pumpkin

Sour Cream Topping (right)

Preheat oven to 325°F. Place melted butter in the bottom of a 10-inch spring form pan. Press crushed ginger snaps into the butter. Set aside.

Beat cream cheese, sugar and spices on low until well mixed, stopping to scrap down the bowl several times. Add eggs one at a time, scraping down the bowl between each addition. Add brandy and maple syrup and scrape down the bowl. Add cream and pumpkin and mix. Gently pour into the spring form pan over the crust. Bake for 1½ hours or until a knife inserted in the center comes out clean. Cool completely before topping with Sour Cream Topping to within a half an inch of the edge. Chill for at least 4 hours before serving. Once topping has set, run a knife around the edge of the cheesecake and remove the outer ring of the spring form pan. Serves 12.

Sour Cream Topping

1 cup sour cream
2 tablespoons sugar
½ teaspoon vanilla

Whisk all ingredients together and then pour over the top of a cooled cheesecake. Chill for at least 4 hours before serving.

Banana Cheesecake

3 tablespoon unsalted butter, melted
4½ ounces chocolate wafer cookies, crushed or ground in a food processor

1½ pounds cream cheese, softened
1¼ cups sugar
½ teaspoon salt
5 eggs
3 bananas, mashed or pureed in a food processor
2 teaspoons fresh lemon juice
½ cup heavy cream
1 teaspoon vanilla

Sour Cream Topping (page 50)

Preheat oven to 325°F. Place melted butter in the bottom of a 10-inch spring form pan. Press crushed chocolate wafer cookies into the butter. Set aside.

Beat cream cheese until very soft. Add sugar and salt and continue to beat, stopping to scrap down the bowl at least once. Add eggs one at a time and scrape down the bowl between each addition. Add the bananas and lemon juice to the creamed mixture and mix thoroughly, stopping to scrape down the bowl at least once while incorporating. Add heavy cream and vanilla and then mix. Pour into the prepared crust in the spring form pan. Bake for 1 to 1½ hours or until a knife inserted into the center comes out clean. Cool completely before topping with Sour Cream Topping to within a half an inch of the edge, chill for at least 4 hours before serving. Once the topping has set, run a knife around the edge of the cheesecake and remove the outer ring from the spring form pan. Serves 12.

White Chocolate Raspberry Cheesecake

3 tablespoon unsalted butter, melted
1 cup graham cracker crumbs

11 ounces white chocolate, chopped
1¼ pounds cream cheese, room temperature
¾ cup sugar
1 tablespoon cornstarch
½ teaspoon salt
1½ teaspoons vanilla
3 eggs
1¼ cups sour cream
1 cup fresh raspberries or ½ cup raspberry preserves or Raspberry Sauce (right)
approximately 1½ cups white chocolate shavings (see Making Chocolate Shavings page 12)

Raspberry Sauce

10 ounces frozen raspberries
¼ cup sugar
½ cup current jelly or raspberry jam
2 tablespoons quick cooking tapioca

Combine all ingredients in a saucepan. Allow to sit for 15 minutes. Heat to boiling and reduce to simmer. Simmer for 5 to 8 minutes. Allow to cool completely before topping cheesecake.

Chunky Raspberry Sauce

Once sauce is finished simmering gently stir in another 10 ounces of whole frozen raspberries or 1 pint fresh raspberries.

Preheat oven to 250°F. Place melted butter in the bottom of a 10-inch spring form pan. Press graham cracker crumbs into the butter. Set aside.

Melt white chocolate in a large bowl over a pan of gently simmering water. Stir occasionally with a rubber spatula, do not allow it to scorch on the bottom of the bowl.

Cream cream cheese and sugar on low speed of mixer. Add cornstarch, salt and vanilla. Scrape bowl down. Add eggs one at a time, scraping down the bowl between each addition. Add sour cream. Add half of cream cheese mixture to the melted white chocolate and stir until combined. Return the white chocolate mixture to the cream cheese mixture in small amounts and scrape down the bowl after each addition.

Gently pour cheesecake batter into the prepared spring form pan and bake for 1¾ to 2 hours or until the center has set. Cool completely before running a knife around the edge of the cheesecake and removing the outer ring of the spring form pan. Top with raspberry preserves or Raspberry Sauce in the center and white chocolate shavings around the edges.

Fruit Pastries, Pies & Tarts

Fresh Fruit Tart [page 63]

Baking Pure & Simple

Fruit Pastries, Pies & Tarts

This apple cake is really more of a tart. My Grandma Lisl used to make it for special occasions. She always called it "Apple Cake"

German Apple Cake

1 recipe Sweet German Crust (right)
4 egg whites
4 egg yolks
¾ cup sugar
2 teaspoons cinnamon
4 Granny Smith apples, cored and sliced thin

Preheat oven to 325°F. Prepare two shallow, 10-inch tart pans with removable bottoms with Sweet German Crust per the recipe.

With an electric mixer, whisk the egg whites until stiff and set aside. In a separate bowl of the electric mixer, whisk the egg yolks until they are thick and pale in color, about 5 minutes, then fold them together with the whites by hand. Mix apple slices, sugar, and cinnamon together. Fold the apples and egg mixture together. Place half of the apple and egg mixture into each tart pan prepared with the unbaked Sweet German Crust. Bake for 40 to 45 minutes or until golden brown. Makes 2 cakes, each serving 8 to 10.

Note: It is best not to make this as a half recipe. If you do only want one cake, divide the apples by half but use 3 eggs, ½ cup sugar and 1½ teaspoons cinnamon.

Sweet German Crust

2 cups flour
¼ cup sugar
½ cup unsalted butter, chilled
1 egg, beaten
1½ tablespoons vegetable oil

Combine flour and sugar. Using your fingers or a pastry cutter, cut the butter into the flour and sugar, until crumbly. Add the egg and oil and mix together with your hands until it resembles pie dough. Divide the dough in half and shape each half into a disk; set one half aside. Roll one disk into a thin layer and place it in a shallow fluted 10-inch tart pan with a removable bottom. The best way to transfer it from the rolling surface to the tart shell is to fold it in half with a bench scraper, making sure it is not sticking to the rolling surface. Next, in a single motion, lift it into the tart pan with the center crease at the center of the pan. Unfold the pastry and gently form it into place in the pan. It will crack and break but just use excess pieces which hang over the edge to fix any holes. Press the edges of the dough into the corners and cut the top of the dough off with a knife or your fingers to make it flush with the top edges of the tart pan. Repeat with the other half of the dough in another tart pan. This dough may be frozen. Makes 2 10-inch tart shells.

Pear or Apples Frangipane Tart

1 recipe German Sweet Crust (page 59)
3 cups dry beans or rice or pie weights for pre-baking tart shells

½ cup unsalted butter, room temperature
½ cup sugar
2 eggs
1 egg yolk
¾ cup ground almonds
2 tablespoons flour
1 tablespoon Kirsh (optional)
3 to 4 pears or apples, washed and dried

½ cup apricot jelly or preserves
¼ cup sliced almonds, lightly toasted

Preheat oven to 350°F. Prepare two shallow, 10-inch tart pans with removable bottoms with Sweet German Crust per the recipe. Line the empty pastry shells with aluminum foil and fill them with dry beans or rice. Push the beans or rice up around the sides of the tart shell to keep the sides from falling during pre-baking. Pre-bake the empty tart shells for 10 minutes. Remove the foil and contents immediately once the tart shells are out of the oven. Allow them to cool slightly.

Cream butter and sugar. Add the eggs one at a time, scraping down the bowl each time and waiting until each addition is fully incorporated before adding the next. Add the egg yolk and scrape down the bowl. Add almonds, flour and Kirsh, if included, and mix on medium speed just until combined. Chill the mixture for a few minutes while you prepare the fruit.

Slice pears or apples into quarters and then slice out the seed casings before slicing each quarter into quarters again. Check the length of a slice to see if it comes to about the middle of the pastry shell in the tart pan. If it is too long slice a small portion off the top of every other slice.

Spread half of the frangipane mixture into each partially baked tart shell as evenly as possible. Arrange the fruit in a circular pattern. Alternate long and short slices and arrange fruit so that the thinner end is in the middle. Bake for 40 to 45 minutes until the frangipane filling is nicely brown and has puffed up between the fruit slices. Cool completely.

Melt apricot preserves with a tablespoon of water in a small saucepan until bubbly. Brush over the tart and sprinkle the toasted sliced almonds across the top for garnish. Makes 2 10-inch tarts, each serving 8 to 10.

This tart is made in a 12-inch tart pan with a removable bottom. Select only the most beautiful fresh fruit when making a fresh fruit tart and consider a variety of colors.

Fresh Fruit Tart

½ recipe Cartier Crust dough (page 66)
½ recipe Custard, (page 103, cooled completely)
3 cups ripe, beautiful strawberries, hulled and sliced in half
1 half pint raspberries
1 half pint blueberries
2 kiwi fruits, peeled and sliced
4 ripe apricots, stones removed, cut into thin slices
3 tablespoons melted chocolate or Ganache at room temperature (page 33)

Preheat oven to 350°F. Press the Cartier Crust dough to a uniform thickness of just under a quarter inch into the bottom of a tart pan with a fluted edge and a removable bottom. Be careful not to make the corner edges thicker than the bottom and sides. Poke the crust with a fork on the bottom in several places. Bake 15 to 20 minutes or until lightly brown. You may need to release air bubbles during baking by poking the crust with a fork again. Allow to the tart shell to cool completely. Leave the tart shell in the pan during finishing.

Using the back of a spoon, spread the Ganache or chocolate in a very thin layer on the baked, cooled crust. Chill the tart shell until the chocolate has set up or the Ganache is solid before the next step. Place the custard into a bowl and whisk by hand or with an electric mixer until very smooth, small lumps may remain. Using a large spoon, gently fill the prepared tart shell with custard. It should come to just about a quarter inch beneath the top edge of the crust. You may have leftover custard.

Carefully wash the fruit and dry it with paper towel. You may want to skip washing the raspberries, as they may bleed juice which is not good for the presentation. Arrange the fruit in concentric circles starting at the outer edge of the tart shell and working toward the center. Vary the color and shape of the fruit using the smaller fruit as you approach the center. Assemble the tart just before serving if possible. If you need to put it together prior to serving, refrigerate until ready to serve. Remove the outer ring of the tart shell just before presenting. Use a serrated knife to slice. Clean the knife between each cut. Serves 12.

Note: You can bake the crust and make the custard the day before serving. At least make the custard the day before so it can cool completely.

This torte is best if made the day before it is served.

Raspberry Rhapsody

1¾ to 2 cups unbaked Cartier Crust dough (page 66)
¾ cup raspberry preserves
4 eggs
1 cup loosely packed brown sugar
2 cups walnuts, chopped
½ cup coconut
2 tablespoons oatmeal, chopped

Preheat oven to 350°F. Press unbaked Cartier Crust dough into a 10-inch round spring form pan. Spread ⅓ cup of the raspberry preserves into a thin layer over the Cartier Crust to within a ¼-inch of the side of the pan. Combine eggs and brown sugar and whip on high speed of mixer until thick and fluffy, 5 to 10 minutes. Fold in walnuts, coconut and oatmeal. Pour the mixture over the top of the preserves. Bake for 40 to 45 minutes, until very brown and a wooden pick inserted in the center comes out dry. Do not under bake. The center may fall slightly while cooling.

When completely cool run a knife around the edge of the pan all the way to the bottom, then remove outer spring form. Spread the remaining raspberry preserves onto the top of the cake in a thin layer to within an inch of the outer edge. Cut a piece of cake cardboard to the size of the circle of raspberry preserves. Lay it over the raspberry preserves and dust the edges of the cake with powdered sugar. Remove the cardboard. While slicing for service, clean the knife under hot water and dry it before each cut. Serves 12.

Raspberry Rhapsody Bars

To make Raspberry Rhapsody Bars in a 13 by 9-inch baking pan, use 3 cups of Cartier Crust and ½ cup of raspberry preserves. Follow the directions for the remaining ingredients. Bake at 350°F for 30 to 40 minutes or until a toothpick comes out clean. Cool completely.

Cut into 18 squares. While slicing for service, clean the knife under hot water and dry it before each cut. Dust the bars with powdered sugar before serving, if desired. Pictured on page 162.

Chocolate Banana or Strawberry Cartier

12 Chocolate Cartier crust barquettes or small tarts, baked, cooled and removed from pans
½ recipe Chocolate Mousse (page 31) from Chocolate Flourless Cake, chilled
2 to 3 ripe bananas, sliced about ¼ inch thick or 1 quart medium strawberries, cut in half
½ pound semi-sweet chocolate, melted and cooled slightly
1 tablespoon vegetable oil

> ***Warning:*** *The mousse in these Cartiers contains raw eggs. Some people may not wish to consume raw eggs and should use the Soft Chocolate Ganache on (page 33) instead of the Chocolate Mousse. Make the ganache the day before you plan to use it, so it will have time to set up.*

Fill a pastry bag without a tip in it or a plastic freezer bag with ½ inch tip of the corner cut out with chocolate mousse. Pipe into the baked Cartier crusts to the level of the top of the barquette or tart edge. Layer with sliced bananas or strawberries, slightly overlapping. Combine chocolate with vegetable oil until smooth. Brush chocolate over the bananas or strawberries until they are coated. Refrigerate until the chocolate is solid. Keep refrigerated until just before serving. Makes 12 Cartiers.

Cartier Crust

1 cup unsalted butter, room temperature
1¼ cups loosely packed brown sugar
1 egg
3 cups flour
1 cup walnuts, chopped

Preheat oven to 350°F. Cream butter and brown sugar. Add egg. Blend in flour. Add nuts. Use your hands to press into a dough that holds together.

Press into tart pans with removable bottoms or into individual barquette molds or tart pans.
Bake until lightly brown, about 15 to 20 minutes. Makes 6 cups of dough.

Chocolate Cartier Crust: Reduce flour to 2½ cups and add ⅔ cup cocoa.

Pâte Brisée

2 cups flour
½ teaspoon sugar
½ teaspoon salt
7 ounces unsalted butter, chilled (1 cup less 2 tablespoons)
1 egg
1 tablespoon plus 1 teaspoon milk

Mix flour, sugar and salt together. Using your hands, cut in butter until mixture is crumbly; small chunks of butter may still be visible. Whisk eggs and milk together in a separate bowl. Add into the flour mixture all at once and mix just until combined. Use your hands to press the mixture together until it is mostly holding its shape with just a few loose areas. Place on a floured board and fold and flatten 4 times. The dough should now be mostly uniform with a few flecks of butter here and there. Press the dough into 6 round disks if making Baked Apples (page 69) or into 2 round disks if using for tarts. Wrap each disk individually in plastic wrap. Chill for at least an hour. Remove from the refrigerator about an hour before using. Makes enough for 6 baked apples or 2 tarts.

Caramel Sauce

6 tablespoons unsalted butter
1⅓ cups brown sugar
1⅓ cups heavy cream, divided

Combine butter, brown sugar and 1 cup of the cream in a sauce pan, reserving remaining cream. Heat to boiling, stirring constantly with a whisk and keeping the whisk in contact with the bottom of the saucepan. Continue cooking for about 5 to 10 minutes until the mixture thickens and browns to a caramel color. Use caution since the mixture will bubble and steam. Continue stirring until the mixture is the desired consistency, adding the remaining cream if necessary. Makes 2 cups.

Note: The sauce may be refrigerated for about a week. To reheat, return to boiling, adding small amounts of cream, until desired thickness is reached.

I love to make these apples at Thanksgiving. One year my sisters were over and I was in a particularly silly mood while finishing them up. I started imitating Julia Child, explaining each step along the way in a loud, high-pitched voice. I always remember that moment when I bake them. They are best if served with French vanilla ice cream.

Baked Apples with Caramel Sauce

1 recipe Pâte Brisée (page 67)
6 small Granny Smith apples, peeled and cored
18 pecan halves
1 teaspoon cinnamon and ½ cup each sugar and brown sugar, mixed
¼ cup raisins
¼ cup pecans, chopped
12 ½-inch chunks of unsalted butter, about ¼ cup
juice of 1 lemon
1 egg, beaten

1 recipe Caramel Sauce (page 67)

Preheat oven to 425°F. Dip the apples in lemon juice as they are peeled and cored. Combine sugar mixture with raisins and chopped pecans. Roll each apple in the sugar mixture. Then place one chunk of butter inside the bottom of the cored apple. Place some of the sugar mixture with the raisins and chopped pecans inside the apple and top with another butter chunk.

Half Size Baked Apples

If you can only find large Granny Smith apples it is a good idea to cut them in half. Follow the instructions, filling where the core would have been with the sugar nut mixture and placing a smaller chunk of butter on each end. Place the apple cut side down on the rolled out pastry dough and wet the edge of the dough all around the perimeter before bringing the edges up to form three sides which meet in the center. Pinch the edges together all the way to make a point at the center top. Fold over the edges and then as you place the apple on the baking sheet fold the edges of the three points of pastry underneath the apple. Brush with the egg as noted. Prick the pastry with a fork on all three sides before baking.

Roll out one of the six Pâte Brisée disks and place the prepared apple in the center of the pastry. Pull up all the sides to enclose the apple at the other end of the core. Wet the edges to seal and pinch to close. Invert the apple so that the sealed edge is down on the baking pan and curve the excess pastry around the sides of the apple, smoothing it gently and tucking any excess underneath. Continue with the remaining apples and Pâte Brisée until all have been wrapped. Cut a small X in the pastry at the top of each apple with a sharp knife. Brush the pastry with beaten egg on the top and sides and bake at 425°F for 10 minutes or until pastry begins to brown. Turn the oven down to 350°F and bake for an additional 20 to 25 minutes until the apples seem to soften. Check them with a sharp knife. While still warm remove the apples to serving platters or plates. Top each with 3 pecan halves and Caramel Sauce just before serving. Best if served warm with French vanilla ice cream. Serves 6.

Note: These apples hold up very well in the refrigerator for a few days. Reheat them before serving for about 20 minutes at 350°F.

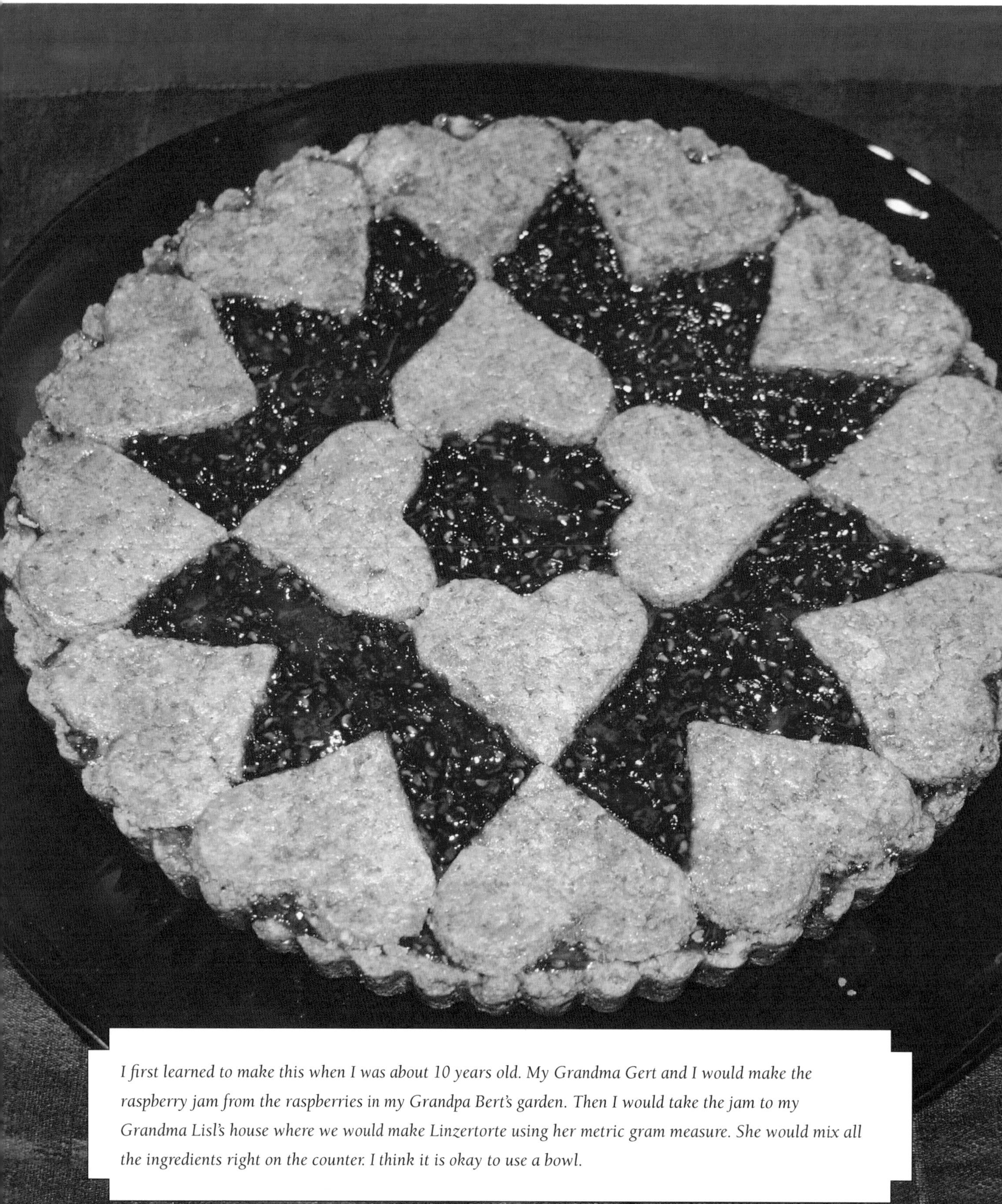

I first learned to make this when I was about 10 years old. My Grandma Gert and I would make the raspberry jam from the raspberries in my Grandpa Bert's garden. Then I would take the jam to my Grandma Lisl's house where we would make Linzertorte using her metric gram measure. She would mix all the ingredients right on the counter. I think it is okay to use a bowl.

Linzertorte

3 cups flour
1 cup unsalted butter
1½ cups sugar
2⅓ cups ground pecans
2 tablespoons cocoa
¼ teaspoon ground cloves
½ teaspoon cinnamon
2 tablespoons whiskey
1 egg, slightly beaten
12 ounces raspberry jam

1 egg slightly beaten for egg wash

Using your hands, cut the butter into the flour until the mixture is crumbly. Add the sugar, nuts, cocoa and spices. Continue to mix with your hands. Add the whiskey and the egg. Mix together and work into ball. Divide the dough into 6 balls and shape each one into flat disks. Chill overnight.

Linzer Hearts

Follow the instructions for the Linzertorte dough, separating it into only 2 balls instead of 6. Roll the dough out as for Linzertorte. Using heart shaped cookie cutters in different sizes cut out one base layer cookie and then another in the same size but with the center removed by cutting it out with a smaller size heart shaped cookie cutter. Place the first heart shaped piece on a cookie sheet, layer with a thin layer of raspberry jam then top with the heart with the center removed. Brush pastry with egg wash. Bake the cookies at 300°F for about 25 to 30 minutes. When slightly cool add more jam in the open center. These are a nice addition to the holiday assortment and are pictured on the holiday cookie tray. These cookies freeze very well. Makes 3 dozen.

Remove the disks of dough from the refrigerator about a hour before beginning to prepare the torte. Preheat oven to 300°F. Roll out one disk to about ¼-inch thickness and place it in a 10-inch tart pan with a removable bottom, pressing together any cracks and pressing up the sides of the pan. Watch that the corners do not become too thick. Spread ¼ cup of the raspberry jam thinly to within a ¼-inch of the edge of the pan. Roll out the second layer of dough and cover the layer of jam. Spread with another ¼ cup of the jam. Roll out the last layer. Cut into strips and make a lattice design with them over the top or cut into heart (or other) shapes and arrange in a pattern over the jam. Repeat with remaining dough in another tart pan. This dough is very fragile, but if you push it together, it heals while baking. Bake for 35 to 40 minutes. Cool slightly then add more jam in the open spaces between the strips or hearts while the torte is still warm.

When the torte is completely cool remove the outer ring of the tart pan. My grandmother always said it was best if stored in the freezer for a few months before serving, but I find that it is okay to serve after a day or two of refrigeration. Be sure to wrap it well in plastic wrap and freezer bags during storage.

Makes 2 10-inch Linzertortes, serving 8 each.

I love the soft, light flavor of this apple and pear cake. It is perfect for fall.

Gateau Anna with Brandy Cream Sauce

2 eggs
¾ cup sugar
1 cup flour
1 tablespoon baking powder
¼ teaspoon salt
2 Granny Smith apples, cored and thinly sliced
2 pears, cored and thinly sliced
½ cup unsalted butter, melted and slightly cooled
1½ tablespoons light rum

Brandy Cream Sauce

Place a cup of Custard (page 103) into a bowl and whisk until smooth. Add 2 tablespoons of brandy and whisk until combined. Add milk or cream a few tablespoons at a time until the mixture is the desired consistency. Makes 1 cup.

Preheat oven to 350°F. Whip eggs and sugar on high speed of an electric mixer until thick and light in color, about 7 minutes. Combine flour, baking powder and salt and sift over the egg mixture. Fold together by hand then fold in the melted butter and rum. Finally, gently fold in the sliced fruit. Bake in a greased 10-inch spring form pan for 45 to 55 minutes or until a knife or wooden pick inserted in the center comes out dry. If after 45 minutes a pick does not come out dry, but the top is sufficiently brown, reduce heat to 325°F for the remaining time or move to a lower shelf in the oven. Cool completely before running a knife around the edge and removing outer spring form side of the pan. Cut into 12 pieces. Sprinkle the top with powdered sugar just before serving. Serve on top of a pool of Brandy Cream Sauce. Serves 12.

Whenever I see the first rhubarb of the season I know summer is coming soon. I always love to make this sweet, tangy treat. In the hotel we would make it as a special for a whole month. It was always a favorite.

Strawberry Rhubarb Pie

2½ cups strawberries, washed, hulled and quartered
2½ cups rhubarb, washed, leaves and roots removed and cut into 1-inch pieces
1½ cups sugar
¼ cup flour
2 tablespoons quick cooking tapioca
2 teaspoons grated orange rind

1 recipe Pie Dough (page 85)
1 egg, beaten
1 teaspoon Turbinado sugar

Preheat oven to 425°F. Roll out the bottom pie dough layer to fit a 9-inch pie pan. Line the pie pan with the dough overlapping the edges by about an inch. Roll out the top layer and set aside.

Combine strawberries, rhubarb, sugar, flour, tapioca and orange rind in a large bowl and toss to mix. Place the fruit into the prepared pie shell. Lightly moisten the edge of the bottom pie crust where it will meet the top crust with water. Lay the top crust over the filling and press the edges together, leaving the extra crust to overhang the edge. Gently tuck the extra crust under the sealed edge just inside the pie pan and crimp the edges with the thumb of one hand and the thumb and forefinger of the other to make a scalloped edge.

Brush top crust with the beaten egg. Cut slits in the top crust at regular intervals with a sharp knife. Sprinkle with Turbinado sugar. Bake the pie on the lower rack of the oven at 425°F for 15 minutes. Turn the oven temperature down to 375°F for 25 to 35 minutes or until the pie is nicely browned and the fruit has just begun to bubble up through the slits in the top crust. Cool completely. Serves 8.

With peaches, ripeness is a factor. You will want peaches that are just a little bit soft when gently squeezed for either the Peach Cream Pie or for the Peach Cobbler. Not too hard, not too soft, just right. Juiciness, ripeness, firmness and color are all factors. The best Peach Cobbler I ever made was made with 3 different kinds of peaches, magenta and yellow peaches mixed with some organic variety. When I was peeling them I knew that some were more ripe and soft than others, but the combination worked out very well. Never use peaches that are so ripe that they seem squishy or fermented, and always cut out any brown spots. July is generally the best time of year for peaches.

Peach Cream Pie

¾ cup sugar
6 tablespoons flour
¼ teaspoon salt
¼ teaspoon nutmeg
½ teaspoon cinnamon
6 cups fresh peaches, peeled, sliced and soaked in ½ cup maple syrup
for 1 to 2 hours then drained
¾ cup whipping cream

1 recipe Pie Dough (page 85)
1 egg, beaten
1 teaspoon Turbinado sugar (optional)

How to Peel Peaches

To peel peaches, make a small X with a sharp knife at the bottom of each peach then submerge them in boiling water for 60 seconds or until you see that the skin is lifting at the X. Remove the peaches from the boiling water with a fork and as soon as you can handle them peel the skins with a small butter knife or your fingers. If the skins do not come off easily, submerge the peaches in the boiling water for another 60 seconds. If they still do not come off, you will have to carefully cut them off. The riper the peaches, the easier the skins will come off. Use caution; the peaches will be slippery.

Preheat oven to 425°F. Roll out bottom pie dough to fit a 10-inch pie pan. Line the pie pan with the dough overlapping the edges by about an inch. Mix sugar, flour, salt, nutmeg and cinnamon together in a bowl. Toss with peaches and place in the pie shell. Pour whipping cream over the top. Lightly moisten the edge of the bottom pie crust where it will meet the top crust with water. Roll out the top pie dough and lay it over the peaches. Press the edges together, leaving the extra crust to overhang the edge. Gently tuck the extra crust under the sealed edge just inside the pie pan and crimp the edges with the thumb of one hand and the thumb and forefinger of the other to make a scalloped edge.

Brush top crust with the beaten egg. Place slits in the top crust with a knife and sprinkle with Turbinado sugar. Bake on the lower rack of the oven at 425°F for 15 minutes, then reduce heat to 375°F for 25 to 35 minutes or until browned. Serves 8.

Peach Cobbler

14 peaches, skins removed (see Peach Cream Pie recipe page 77) and sliced into eighths (about 10 cups)
1 cup brown sugar
1 teaspoon cinnamon
1 teaspoon vanilla
1½ tablespoons flour
1 tablespoon unsalted butter, cut into quarters

2 cups flour
2 teaspoons baking powder
1 teaspoon baking soda
½ cup sugar
½ cup unsalted butter
¾ cup buttermilk

2 tablespoons Turbinado sugar

Preheat oven to 425°F. Combine peaches, brown sugar, cinnamon, vanilla, 1½ tablespoons flour and 1 tablespoon butter and place in a large, deep 14 by 10-inch casserole dish. Place in the oven on the lower rack for 15 to 25 minutes, depending on the ripeness of your peaches, the riper the peaches, the less cooking time required. Leaving the pan in the oven, pull out the rack and stir the peaches at least once during cooking. When the peaches seem soft and the juices are thickened and shinny, remove from the oven to add the topping.

Prepare the cobbler crust while the peaches are in the oven.

In a large bowl combine flour, baking powder, baking soda and sugar. Cut in butter with your hands until the mixture is crumbly. Add buttermilk and mix gently with your hands until the mixture just comes together. Turn the dough out onto a well-floured surface and fold and flatten with your hands 3 or 4 times. Divide the dough into 12 pieces, shape each one into a 2 to 3 inch round patty approximately ½ inch thick. Place them on top of the partially cooked peaches, taking care to leave about an inch of space in between each one on all sides. Brush the top of the dough with the beaten egg and sprinkle with the Tubinano sugar. Return to the center or upper rack of the oven and bake for 15 to 18 minutes until the crust is golden brown. Serves 12-15.

Blueberry Pie

7 cups fresh blueberries
¼ cup quick cooking tapioca
1 cup maple syrup
¼ cup water
pinch of salt
1 teaspoon lime zest
½ tablespoon lime juice

1 recipe Pie Dough (page 85)
1 egg, beaten
1 teaspoon Turbinado sugar (optional)

Wash the blueberries. Puree 1 cup of the berries and combine with the tapioca, maple syrup and water in a saucepan. Stir together and allow to sit for 10 minutes before cooking. Heat to boiling for about 5 minutes. Mixture will get very thick. Combine the remaining blueberries, lime zest, juice and salt in a large bowl. Stir the hot thickened puree into the blueberries and refrigerate for at least an hour or until the mixture is completely chilled.

Preheat oven to 425°F. Roll pie dough out to fit a 10-inch pie pan. Line the pie pan with the dough overlapping the edges by about an inch. Place the chilled blueberry mixture in the shell. Lightly moisten the edge of the bottom pie crust where it will meet the top crust with water. Roll out the top pie dough and place over the blueberries. Press the edges together, leaving the extra crust to overhang the edge. Gently tuck the extra crust under the sealed edge just inside the pie pan and crimp the edges with the thumb of one hand and the thumb and forefinger of the other to make a scalloped edge.

Brush the top of the pie with the beaten egg. Place slits in the top crust with a sharp knife and sprinkle with Turbinado sugar. Bake on the lower oven rack at 425°F for 15 minutes, then reduce heat to 375°F for 25 to 35 minutes or until browned. Serves 8.

Substitute margarine for the butter and this dessert becomes vegan. It is shown here with ice cream, but it is great just on its own. There are vegan ice creams made with Coconut Milk on the market which would make a nice compliment.

Blueberry Crisp

½ cup sugar or maple syrup
3 tablespoons cornstarch
11 cups blueberries, rinsed and drained
1 tablespoon lime juice
1 recipe Oatmeal Crumb Topping (below)

Preheat oven to 375°F. Combine sugar or maple syrup and cornstarch. Add blueberries and lime juice. Pour into a 13 by 9-inch glass or ceramic baking pan. Distribute Oatmeal Crumb Topping over the blueberry mixture. Bake for 35 to 45 minutes or until brown and bubbly. Serve with vanilla ice cream, if desired. Serves 12.

Oatmeal Crumb Topping

3 cups oatmeal
1 cup brown sugar
⅔ cup flour or spelt flour
1½ teaspoons cinnamon
½ cup unsalted butter (or margarine for vegan version)

Combine ingredients by hand until crumbly. Makes 4 cups.

Maple Syrup version: Substitute maple syrup for brown sugar, increase oatmeal to 4 cups, increase flour to ¾ cup.

Strawberry Shortcake

2¼ cups flour
½ cup sugar
1 tablespoon baking powder
1 teaspoon baking soda
¼ teaspoon salt
½ cup unsalted butter, chilled
½ cup buttermilk
1 teaspoon lemon zest
2 eggs, slightly beaten, 2 tablespoons reserved for brushing on shortcakes before baking
2 tablespoons Turbinado sugar

2 quarts strawberries, hulled and sliced
¼ to ½ cup sugar
1 pint whipping cream sweetened with ½ cup powdered sugar and 1½ teaspoons vanilla and whipped, chilled until ready to serve.

Preheat oven to 450°F. Combine flour, ½ cup sugar, baking powder, baking soda and salt in a large bowl. Cut in the butter until the mixture is crumbly. Combine buttermilk, lemon zest and beaten eggs. Mix the wet ingredients into the dry ingredients just until the mixture holds together.

Turn the mixture onto a well-floured board and pat it into an 8-inch square, fold it in half and pat it down again, this time to the same thickness in a rectangle, then fold it in half again back into a square. Finally, pat it down a third time back into an 8-inch square. Divide the dough into 8 equal pieces and shape each one into a circle. Place shortcakes on a greased baking sheet and brush the tops of each one with the reserved beaten egg. Sprinkle the tops with Turbinado sugar. Bake for 10 to 12 minutes or until lightly browned. Remove to cooling racks.

Combine sliced strawberries with the ¼ to ½ cup sugar, to taste. Allow to sit in the refrigerator for at least 30 minutes to an hour, stirring occasionally.

When shortcakes are completely cooled, slice horizontally and place each bottom half in an individual serving bowl. Top each with some of the sliced strawberries, being sure to include some of the juices. Cover strawberries with the upper half of the shortcake, then add more sliced strawberries and a healthy dollop or two of the sweetened whipped cream. Serves 8.

Maple Strawberry Rhubarb Crisp

6 cups diced rhubarb
4 cups quartered strawberries
½ cup flour
⅓ cup quick cooking tapioca
1 cup maple syrup
4 teaspoons orange rind
1 recipe Oatmeal Crumb Topping (page 81)

Preheat oven to 375°F. Toss together rhubarb, strawberries, flour, tapioca, maple syrup and orange rind and place in a 13 by 9-inch baking pan. Top evenly with the Oatmeal Crumb Topping. Bake for 30 to 40 minutes until fruit is bubbly and topping is browned. Serves 12.

Maple Strawberry Rhubarb Crisp is another summer favorite, with or without ice cream. Rhubarb is only around for a short time, be sure to take advantage of it while it is available.

Strawberry Rhubarb Pie [page 75]

Pie Dough

2 cups flour
1 teaspoon salt
2 teaspoons sugar
¼ cup unsalted butter
3 tablespoon vegetable shortening
⅓ to ½ cup water

Combine flour, salt and sugar. Cut in butter and shortening till crumbly. Add water, starting with ⅓ cup and then adding slowly to desired consistency, mixing only until combined.

Divide into two balls (one slightly larger than the other if making an upper and lower crust) and flatten into disks. Seal in plastic wrap and refrigerate a few hours or overnight. Makes 2 bottom pie shells or 1 upper and lower crust. Remove the dough from the refrigerator for 10 minutes before rolling out.

Wheat-free pie crust: Substitute spelt flour for wheat flour.

Tips on Making Pies

Bake empty pie shells at 425°F with a tinfoil liner filled with pie weights or dried beans.

Bake fresh fruit pies on the lower rack of the oven at 425°F for the first 15 minutes then reduce the heat to 375°F for the remaining baking time.

Always cut small openings (slits) with a sharp knife or fork in the top crust of covered pies before baking so that steam can escape.

Seal covered pies by moistening the lower crust where it will meet the top crust with water before crimping top and bottom crusts together.

Make sure fresh fruit pie fillings are thoroughly chilled before filling pie crusts for baking.

Egg wash the top crust of a pie and sprinkle with turbinado sugar just before baking.

Mousses, Trifles & Pâte à Choux

Swans [page 115]

Baking Pure & Simple

Mousses, Trifles & Pâte à Choux

Chocolate Mousse

1 quart heavy cream
11 ounces semi-sweet chocolate, melted in a large bowl over simmering water
½ cup sugar
¼ cup water
6 egg yolks
chocolate covered espresso beans for garnish

Whip cream until very soft peaks form; it should be slightly less whipped then normal. Set aside in the refrigerator.

Heat sugar and water in a small pan until the sugar has dissolved and the mixture is bubbly and thick. Place the yolks in the bowl of an electric mixer and begin whipping on medium speed. Gently pour the hot sugar down the side of the bowl into the yolks while whipping. Once all the sugar is poured in, turn up the speed of the mixer and whip until the yolks turn pale yellow and thick.

Remove the bowl of chocolate from the simmering water. Whisk the egg yolk mixture into the chocolate by hand in three small batches, making sure the mixture is smooth after each addition. Whisk in a small portion of the whipped cream. Finish whipping the cream until normal thickness and then fold it in to the chocolate mixture. Using a pastry bag without any tip, pipe the mousse into glasses or bowls for serving. Mousse may also be spooned into the serving dishes with large spoons. Top each serving with a chocolate espresso bean. Makes 15 servings.

White Chocolate Mousse

Substitute white chocolate for the semi-sweet chocolate. Melt the white chocolate in a metal bowl over very gently simmering water and stir constantly with a rubber spatula. Follow remaining directions.

Carrot Raisin Muffins

½ cup tapioca flour
¼ cup rice flour
¼ cup ground flaxseed
¾ cup oat bran
½ teaspoon salt
1½ teaspoons baking powder
1½ teaspoons baking soda
2 eggs
¾ cup honey
⅓ cup buttermilk
⅓ cup unsalted butter, melted
4 carrots, finely shredded
½ cup golden raisins
1 cup walnuts, chopped

Preheat oven to 400°F. Combine flours, flaxseed, oat bran, salt, baking powder and soda in a large bowl. In a smaller bowl combine eggs, honey, buttermilk and melted butter. Stir the wet ingredients into the dry using as few strokes as possible. Stir in carrots, raisins and walnuts. Bake in greased muffin pans for 20 minutes or until a wooden pick comes out clean. Allow muffins to cool for 10 to 15 minutes before loosening them around the edges with a knife and gently removing them from the pans. Makes 10 muffins.

Blueberry Muffins

¾ cup unsalted butter, melted
2 eggs
½ cup milk
1 teaspoon vanilla
1½ cups flour
⅔ cup sugar
2 teaspoon baking powder
1 teaspoon salt
2 cups blueberries (fresh or frozen)
1 tablespoon flour
¼ recipe Oatmeal Crumb Topping (page 81)

Preheat oven to 400°F. Whisk together melted butter, eggs, milk and vanilla, set aside. Combine flour, sugar, baking powder and salt in a large bowl. Pour the egg mixture into the dry ingredients and combine with a wooden spoon or spatula in as few strokes as possible until almost combined, but still some dry and wet ingredients remain visible. Toss blueberries in the 1 tablespoon flour. Add blueberries to the mixture along with half the Oatmeal Crumb Topping, again using as few strokes as possible to combine. Mixture will not be uniform. Scoop the mixture into greased muffin tins, with batter coming slightly over the top. Sprinkle the top of each muffin with the remaining oatmeal crumb topping. Bake for 25 to 30 minutes or until muffins are lightly brown on top and a wooden pick comes out clean.

Allow muffins to cool slightly before gently inserting a knife beneath the edges of the muffins and carefully removing them from the muffin pan. Makes 8 to 10 muffins, depending on how full you fill the pans.

Note: Remove grease and pour a few tablespoons of water into any empty muffin holders in the pan. It will help keep them from discoloring in the oven.

Corn Muffins

1 cup yellow cornmeal
1 cup flour
¼ cup sugar
1 teaspoon baking soda
2 teaspoons cream of tartar
¾ teaspoon salt
1 cup sour cream
¼ cup milk
2 eggs, beaten
¼ cup unsalted butter, melted
½ cup corn kernels, fresh or frozen
½ jalapeno pepper, finely diced

Preheat oven to 425°F. Mix cornmeal, flour, sugar, baking soda, cream of tartar and salt in a large bowl. In a separate bowl combine the sour cream, milk, eggs and melted butter. Mix the wet ingredients into the dry with a wooden spoon until just blended. Stir in the corn and peppers. Scoop into greased muffin tins and bake for 12 to15 minutes. Allow to cool for 10 to 15 minutes before running a knife around the edge of each muffin and gently removing them from the pan.

Maple Corn Muffins: Substitute maple syrup for the sugar and add ½ cup more cornmeal.

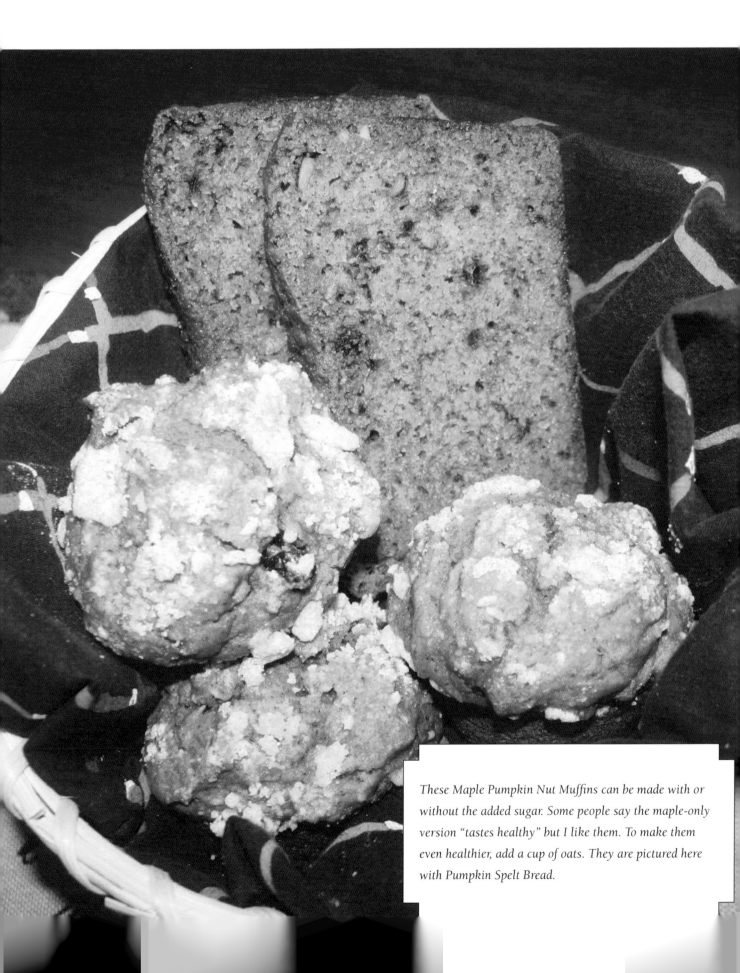

These Maple Pumpkin Nut Muffins can be made with or without the added sugar. Some people say the maple-only version "tastes healthy" but I like them. To make them even healthier, add a cup of oats. They are pictured here with Pumpkin Spelt Bread.

Maple Pumpkin Nut Muffins

2 eggs
1 cup maple syrup
½ cup sugar (optional)
¾ cup vegetable oil
1 15-ounce can pumpkin
3 cups flour
1 teaspoon salt
2 teaspoons baking soda
1½ teaspoons cinnamon
1 teaspoon nutmeg
1 teaspoon cloves
1 teaspoon allspice
1 cup walnuts, chopped
½ cup raisins
1 cup oatmeal (optional)
Streusel Crumb Topping (right)

Streusel Crumb Topping

½ cup flour
⅓ cup sugar
¾ teaspoon cinnamon
2½ tablespoons unsalted butter

Combine flour, sugar and cinnamon in a bowl. Cut in butter with hands until mixture is crumbly. Makes ¾ cups.

Preheat oven to 350°F. Combine eggs, maple syrup, (sugar), oil and pumpkin in a large bowl. Sift together flour, salt, baking soda, cinnamon, nutmeg, cloves and allspice. Combine with wet ingredients just until mixed. Stir in walnuts and raisins (and oatmeal) in as few strokes as possible. Spoon into greased muffin tins and top with Streusel Crumb Topping. Bake for 18 to 23 minutes or until a wooden pick inserted in the center comes out clean. Cool at least 20 minutes before gently running a knife around the edge of each muffin and carefully removing the muffins from the pan. Makes 12 muffins.

Low-Fat Applesauce Bran Muffins

2¼ cups whole wheat or spelt flour
3½ cups wheat bran
½ teaspoon salt
1½ teaspoons baking soda
1 tablespoon orange zest, grated
⅓ cup orange juice
3½ cups unsweetened applesauce
2 eggs
¾ cup molasses
¼ cup vegetable oil
¾ cup raisins
1 cup walnuts, chopped

Preheat oven to 375°F. Combine flour, bran, salt and baking soda in a large bowl. In a smaller bowl combine orange zest and juice, applesauce, eggs, molasses and oil. Stir the wet ingredients into the dry using as few strokes as possible. Stir in the raisins and walnuts. Bake in greased muffin pans almost full for 18 to 22 minutes or until a wooden pick comes out clean. Makes 18 muffins. The batter may also be baked in 2 greased 5 by 9-inch loaf pans for 40 to 45 minutes.

Wheat-free version: Substitute oat bran for wheat bran and coconut flour for whole wheat flour. Add 1 cup of flaxseed. Bake as directed.

Lemon Apricot Bran Muffins: Substitute ½ - ¾ cup Lemon Curd (page 28) for the orange juice and grated lemon zest for the orange zest. Reduce applesauce to 2 cups and add 1 cup unsweetened prune juice. Substitute agave for molasses and chopped dried apricots for raisins. Bake at 350°F instead of 375°F.

I love these healthy muffins. I used to make them at Debbie and Pat's gourmet food shop in West Bloomfield, Michigan in the late 1980s I was also pretty much addicted to espresso coffee at the time and would have at least one of these muffins for breakfast every day along with a pot of espresso coffee. Good times. The Lemon Apricot Bran Muffins were a result of a refrigerator clean-up. I started out to make the muffins straightaway, then remembered I had leftover lemon curd and lemon zest and found I did not have enough applesauce. In the end, all those polled agreed that they were book worthy. The Low-Fat Applesauce Bran Muffins are pictured on page 116.

Bran Muffins

1¼ cups whole wheat flour or 1½ cups spelt flour
1 teaspoon baking soda
½ teaspoon salt
1½ cups wheat bran
¼ cup ground flaxseed
4 tablespoons unsalted butter, melted
1 egg
¼ cup brown sugar
3 tablespoons molasses
1½ cups buttermilk
½ cup raisins, golden or regular, soaked for a few minutes in hot water and drained
½ cup drained canned crushed pineapple (optional)

Preheat oven to 375°F. Mix dry ingredients and raisins in a bowl. Make a well in the center. Mix wet ingredients in the center. Combine wet and dry ingredients just until mixed. Fill greased muffin tins and bake for 15 to 18 minutes or until a wooden pick inserted in the center comes out clean. Remove muffins while still warm by gently prying them from the muffin tins and place them on a cooling rack. Makes 11 muffins.

Oat Bran Blueberry Muffins

2½ cups oat bran
½ cup ground flaxseed
1 teaspoon cinnamon
½ teaspoon salt
1 teaspoon baking soda
⅔ cup brown sugar
1½ cups buttermilk
4 tablespoons unsalted butter, melted
1 egg
1 teaspoon vanilla
2 cups frozen blueberries
1 cup oatmeal

Preheat oven to 350°F. Combine oat bran, flaxeed, cinnamon, salt, baking soda and brown sugar in a large bowl. Mix buttermilk, melted butter, egg and vanilla together. Add wet ingredients into the dry ingredients and stir just until combined. Stir in blueberries and oatmeal. Scoop into greased muffin tins. Bake for 18 to 22 minutes or until edges are brown and a wooden pick inserted in the center comes out clean. Allow to cool about 10 minutes. Remove muffins while still warm by running a knife around the edge and gently prying them from the muffin tins. Makes 13 muffins.

Banana Nut Bread

½ cup unsalted butter
¾ cup sugar
2 eggs
4 medium or 3 large ripe bananas, mashed or pureed
1 teaspoon vanilla
2 cups flour
1 teaspoon baking soda
½ teaspoon salt
3 tablespoons buttermilk
½ cup walnuts or pecans, chopped

Preheat oven to 325°F. Cream butter and sugar. Add eggs, bananas and vanilla. Sift flour, soda and salt together. Add to the creamed mixture alternately with buttermilk. Add nuts. Bake in a greased and floured 5 by 9-inch loaf pan for 60 to 70 minutes or until a wooden pick inserted in the center comes out clean. Cool completely before removing from the pan. Makes 1 loaf.

Gluten-free version: Substitute 2¼ c. gluten-free baking mix (page 8) for the flour and ¾ cup maple syrup for the sugar. Omit butter milk.

Pumpkin Spelt Bread

Pictured on page 126

3 eggs
2 cups sugar
7½ ounces canned pumpkin
¾ cup vegetable or canola oil
⅓ cup water
1 teaspoon baking powder
2 teaspoon baking soda
1 teaspoon salt
1 teaspoon ground cloves
1 teaspoon cinnamon
2½ cups spelt flour
¾ cup chopped walnuts

Preheat oven to 300°F. In a large bowl combine eggs, sugar, pumpkin, oil and water. In a separate bowl stir together baking powder, baking soda, salt, cloves, cinnamon and flour. Combine the wet ingredients with the dry and stir just until mixed. Stir in the walnuts. Bake in 2 greased non-stick 4 by 8-inch loaf pans for 40 to 50 minutes with a pan of water along side the loaves in the oven. Bread is done when a wooden pick inserted in the center comes out clean. Cool completely before removing from the pans. Makes 2 loaves.

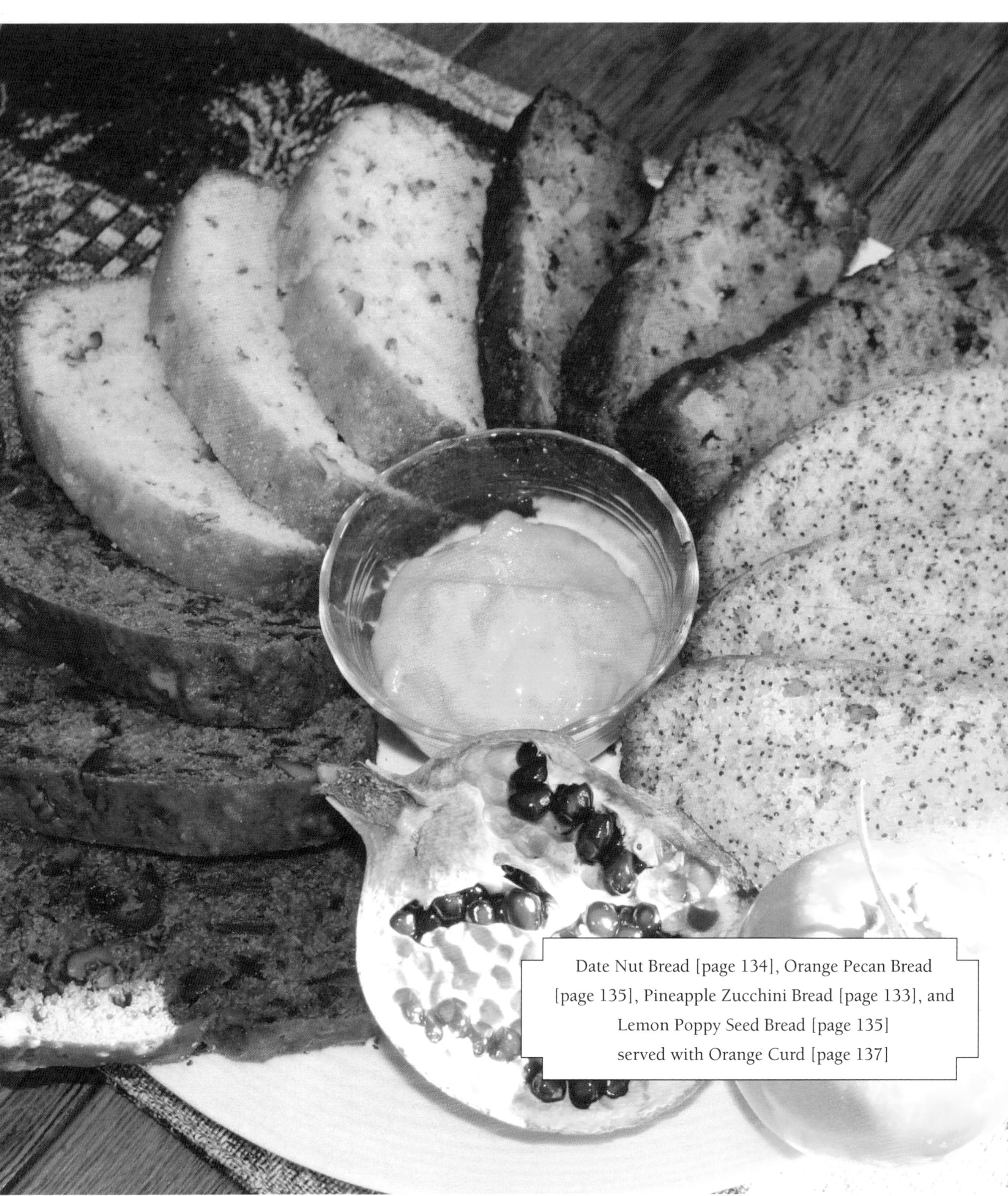

Date Nut Bread [page 134], Orange Pecan Bread [page 135], Pineapple Zucchini Bread [page 133], and Lemon Poppy Seed Bread [page 135] served with Orange Curd [page 137]

Pineapple Zucchini Bread

3 cups flour
1 teaspoon salt
1 teaspoon allspice
1 tablespoon cinnamon
2 teaspoons baking soda
¼ teaspoon baking powder
1¾ cups sugar
1 20-ounce can crushed unsweetened pineapple with juice
3 eggs
½ cup vegetable oil
½ cup unsalted butter, melted
1 tablespoon vanilla
3 cups grated zucchini
1 cup chopped walnuts
½ cup raisins

Preheat oven to 325°F. Stir together flour, salt, allspice, cinnamon, baking soda, baking powder and sugar in a large bowl and make a well in the center. In a separate bowl combine pineapple and its juice, eggs, oil, melted butter and vanilla. Add wet ingredients to the dry ingredients and combine. Add zucchini, nuts and raisins. Stir just until combined. Divide evenly between two greased 5 by 9-inch loaf pans with cornmeal sprinkled on the bottom. Bake for approximately 1 hour or until a wooden pick comes out clean. Cool in pans for at least 30 minutes. Run a knife around the edge of the pan and shake the pan to see if the loaf is free before inverting it into your palm. Turn loaves right side up and place on a cooling rack to finish cooling. Makes 2 loaves.

Date Nut Bread

Pictured on page 132

8 ounces pitted dates, chopped
1 cup boiling water
¼ cup brown sugar
¼ cup unsalted butter
1 egg
¼ cup molasses
2 cups flour
1 teaspoon baking soda
½ teaspoon salt
¾ cup chopped walnuts

Pour the boiling water over the dates and let stand for 1 hour.

Preheat oven to 300F. Cream butter and brown sugar. Add the egg and molasses and continue to cream. Add dates and water to creamed mixture, stirring until just combined. Sift dry ingredients and add to creamed mixture. Stir in nuts. Place batter into a greased 5 by 9-inch loaf pan and allow to stand for 10 minutes before baking for 50 minutes or until a pick inserted into the center comes out clean. Cool completely before removing from the pan. Makes 1 loaf.

Lemon Nut Bread

¾ cup vegetable oil
1¼ cup sugar
2 eggs
1 to 1½ teaspoons lemon zest
1 tablespoon fresh lemon juice
1½ cups flour
1 teaspoon baking powder
½ teaspoon salt
½ cup milk
½ cup chopped walnuts

¼ cup sugar
juice of 1 lemon or orange

Preheat oven to 325°F. Mix oil and sugar with an electric mixer. Add eggs, lemon juice and zest. Combine flour with salt and baking powder. With mixer on slow speed, alternately add the flour mixture and milk to the oil and sugar mixture. Do not over mix. Mix in nuts. Bake in a greased 5 by 9-inch loaf pan (flour just the bottom of the pan) for approximately 1 hour or until a wooden pick inserted in the center comes out clean. Cool about 30 minutes before removing from the pan. Run a knife around the edge of the pan and shake the pan a little to make sure the loaf is free before inverting into your palm. Turn loaf right side up and place on a cooling rack to finish cooling.

Optional Topping: Combine the ¼ cup sugar and lemon juice. Drizzle over the bread when it comes out of the oven.

Lemon Coconut Nut Bread: Add 1 cup unsweetened shredded coconut.

Lemon Poppy Seed Bread: Substitute ¼ cup poppy seeds for the nuts, pictured on page 132.

Lemon Poppy Seed Oat Bran Muffins: Substitute ¼ cup poppy seeds for the nuts and add 2 cups oat bran. Fill greased muffin tins ¾ full. Bake for 20 to 25 minutes or until a wooden pick inserted in the center comes out clean. Makes 11 muffins. Pictured on page 118.

Orange Pecan Bread: Substitute orange zest and juice for the lemon zest and juice and pecans for the walnuts, pictured on page 132.

Gingerbread

½ cup unsalted butter
1 cup dark molasses
½ cup brown sugar
1 cup buttermilk
¼ cup orange juice
2 eggs
3 cups cake flour
1 tablespoon ground ginger
½ teaspoon cinnamon
½ teaspoon nutmeg
½ teaspoon cloves
1 teaspoon salt
1 teaspoon baking soda

1 recipe Orange Curd (right)

Preheat oven to 325°F. Melt butter with molasses and brown sugar in a saucepan. Cool slightly. Combine buttermilk, orange juice and eggs. Sift dry ingredients. Add to the molasses brown sugar mixture alternately with wet ingredients each time using as few strokes as possible. Bake in two greased 5 by 9-inch loaf pans (grease the pans and flour just the bottoms) for 30 to 40 minutes or until a wooden pick inserted in the center comes out clean. Cool for about 20 minutes. Run a knife around the edge of the pans and shake each pan a little to make sure the loaves are free before inverting into your palm. Turn loaf right side up and place on a cooling rack to finish cooling. When fully cool, slice into squares or slices, and serve with Orange Curd. Serves 8 to 10.

Orange Curd

⅜ cup fresh orange juice
zest of 1 orange
½ cup sugar
6 egg yolks
¼ cup unsalted butter

In top of double boiler combine juice, zest, sugar and egg yolks. Cook until thick while stirring constantly, about 15 minutes. Once the mixture has thickened, stir in the butter. Cool completely in refrigerator, stirring occasionally. Chill until serving. Makes 2 cups.

Scones

3¼ cups flour
⅜ cup sugar
1½ tablespoons baking powder
1¼ teaspoons nutmeg
¾ teaspoon salt
¾ cup unsalted butter, chilled
¾ cup heavy cream
3 eggs
1¼ cups currants

Use your imagination to come up with all kinds of scones. Here are just a few ideas to get you started. Traditional Scones with currants, Orange Scones and the Cinnamon Walnut Scones are all pictured on page 116.

1 tablespoon heavy cream mixed with 1 egg
2 tablespoons Turbidano sugar

Preheat oven to 425°F. Sift flour, sugar and baking powder into a large bowl. Using your hands, cut the butter into the mixture until crumbly. Add currants. Mix cream with eggs and add to the mixture, stirring just until combined. Turn onto a lightly floured board. Knead by folding and flattening gently 4 or 5 times. Roll out to ¾-inch thickness. Cut into triangles about 3 inches per side. Brush with the egg and cream mixture. Sprinkle with the Turbidano sugar crystals. Bake for 10 to 12 minutes or until lightly browned. Makes 12 scones.

Orange or Lemon Scones: Add ¼ cup sugar to the dry ingredients, omit the nutmeg and currants and add 1½ tablespoons grated orange or lemon zest. Offer Lemon Scones with Lemon Curd (page 28). Glaze Orange Scones with Butter Cookie Icing (page 157) flavored with orange zest.

Cinnamon Walnut Scones: Substitute 1 tablespoon cinnamon for the nutmeg and walnuts for the currents.

Ginger Scones: Substitute ¼ cup finely diced crystallized ginger for the currants and omit the nutmeg.

Chocolate Chunk Oat Bran Scones: Substitute chocolate chunks for currants and substitute cinnamon for nutmeg. Increase butter by 2 tablespoons, substitute buttermilk for heavy cream and increase by ¼ cup and add 1 cup oat bran.

Dried Cherry or Cranberry Scones: Substitute dried cherries or cranberries for the currents. Substitute cinnamon for the nutmeg. Add 1½ teaspoons grated orange zest (optional). Add 1 cup chopped walnuts or pecans (optional).

Banana Bread Pudding with Chocolate Sauce

4 ounces cream cheese
3 cups milk
3 eggs, beaten
½ cup sugar
1 teaspoons vanilla
1 loaf Banana Nut Bread (page 131), diced into ¾ inch cubes, approximately 6 cups
¼ recipe Sweet Soft Chocolate Ganache Glaze (page 33)

Preheat oven to 350°F. Melt cream cheese in a saucepan over low heat. Slowly whisk in the milk a little at a time. Add eggs, sugar and vanilla and whisk just until combined. Add Banana Nut Bread cubes and allow to stand for 10 minutes. Pour the mixture into a 10 by 14-inch casserole dish. Bake for 45 to 50 minutes or until a knife inserted into the center and gently pulled to one side does not cause uncooked custard to fill in the gap. Allow to cool for at least an hour. Scoop onto serving plates and drizzle with Sweet Soft Chocolate Ganache Glaze.

Blueberry Bread Pudding

3 cups milk
2 cups half and half
4 eggs, beaten
½ cup sugar
1½ teaspoons vanilla
1 teaspoon lemon zest or cinnamon
1 loaf French Bread (page 145) or store bought Challah or egg bread, diced into 6 cups of ¾-inch cubes
1 pint fresh blueberries, divided into 1½ cups and ½ cup
2 tablespoons Turbidano sugar

Preheat oven to 350°F. Combine milk, half and half, eggs, sugar and vanilla. Add bread cubes and allow to stand for 10 to 20 minutes. Wash, drain and dry the blueberries. Place the 1½ cups blueberries into the bottom of a baking dish or divide between 4 to 6 individual baking dishes. Pour or ladle the French Bread mixture into the baking dish or dishes. Sprinkle the reserved blueberries over the top, then sprinkle with the Turbidano sugar. Bake for 45 to 50 minutes in individual dishes or to approximately an hour for a larger baking dish. Test for doneness by inserting a knife into the center of the bread pudding and gently pulling it to one side to see if any uncooked custard fills the gap around the knife. If it does not, then the bread pudding is done. Cool for about 10 minutes if in individual dishes. May be served warm or cooled. The bread pudding will fall back in the center as it cools.

Chocolate Bread Pudding: Substitute chocolate milk for milk, omit blueberries and lemon zest and reduce cinnamon to ½ teaspoon. Add 1 cup semi-sweet chocolate chunks and ¼ teaspoon cayenne pepper.

Brioche

2 tablespoons warm water
2 teaspoons quick rising yeast
3 cups bread flour
2 tablespoons sugar
1 teaspoon salt
5 eggs, beaten
½ cup heavy cream, which has been brought to a boil and cooled
⅔ cup unsalted butter, room temperature and completely softened

1 egg, beaten
1 teaspoon water

Place water in the bowl of a mixer and sprinkle yeast over the water. Add beaten eggs to the cooled cream and whisk until blended. Mix flour, sugar, salt, eggs and cream into the water and yeast with a dough hook or wooden spoon just until blended. Turn onto a floured board and roll out to ¼-inch thickness. Spread softened butter over the dough and fold the dough into quarters. Place in a bowl and cover with a clean towel. Let rise until double, about 2 hours depending on the temperature in the room. I often put the dough in the furnace room with a piece of plastic wrap and a towel over the top. The dough will rise more quickly in a warm place. Once the dough has doubled, refrigerate overnight.

Remove dough from the refrigerator and shape into balls about ¾ the size of the muffin tin and make a hole in the center with your finger. Make a smaller ball of dough and form it into a cone shape, then put it into the hole in the brioche. Repeat with the remaining dough. Allow brioche to rise until double, about 2 to 3 hours, in a warm place. Brush with beaten egg mixed with water. About half an hour before the dough is finished rising, preheat oven to 400°F. Bake for 12 to 14 minutes or until brown. Makes 1 dozen.

Sticky Pecan Brioche Rolls: Melt ¼ cup unsalted butter and combine with ½ cup brown sugar and ¼ cup honey. Smear into the bottom of a 13 by 9-inch baking pan and sprinkle with ½ cup broken pecans. After the dough has rested in the refrigerator overnight, roll it out to a 15 by 11-inch rectangle and brush with 1 tablespoon melted butter. Sprinkle with cinnamon and sugar and dot with raisins. Starting with the long edge, roll the dough up jellyroll style. Slice into 12 pieces, each approximately 1¼ inches long, and place them evenly spaced with the cut side down on top of the brown sugar mixture in the pan. Cover the pan with a clean towel and set it in a warm place for 1½ hours or until rolls have doubled in size. About half an hour before the dough is finished rising, preheat oven to 400°F. Bake for 15 to 18 minutes or until brown. Remove pan from the oven and invert onto a large cookie sheet. Shake the pan gently to loosen all the pecans and caramelized sugar. Remove the baking pan and return the cookie sheet to the oven to finish browning on top for 3 minutes if necessary. Makes 1 dozen.

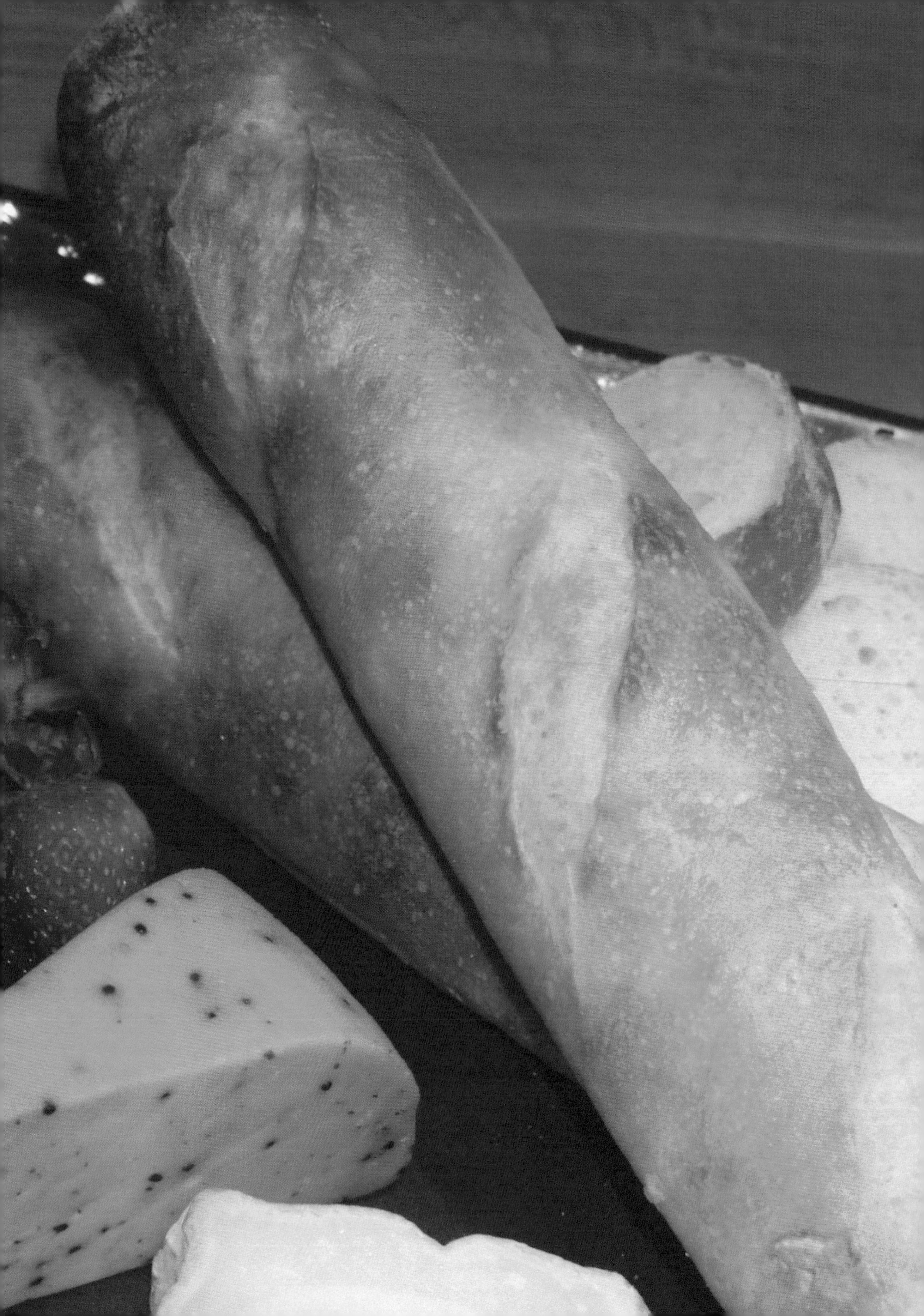

Making French Bread

The best thing about this recipe is how easy it is to make. Just start one day before you want the bread. For example, you can make the dough in the evening after work one day, let it rise until going to bed. Put it in the refrigerator overnight, then take it out the next morning or evening, make the loaves and let them rise and bake them in just a few hours. You can be a hero by bringing French bread to work or just have it all for yourself. The bread freezes very well if wrapped air tight. I often cut loaves in half and fit them into freezer bags. To reheat the frozen loaves, wrap them individually in aluminum foil and bake at 350°F for about 20 minutes.

This quantity will make either 2 large loaves or 2 crusts for homemade 14-inch pizzas. If making the dough for pizza, follow the instructions up to the forming of the loaves, then form your pizza crust on a lightly oiled and cornmeal dusted pan and add sauce, toppings and cheese. Bake the pizza at 450°F.

Essential equipment for making French bread:
French bread pans for 2 long loaves
A plastic bowl scraper
A metal bench scraper
A pizza stone

When I worked in the bakery we would take out the French bread dough first thing in the morning, around 6 a.m. We would heat up the big pizza ovens that we used for just about everything and cut the dough into uniform pieces, weighing each one before putting them through the press. The press would roll them into beautiful loaves that we would place in pans to proof before baking. We had a "proofer" which was a humidity and temperature controlled box for helping bread rise. The bread would be ready for the oven in less than an hour. By 7:30 a.m. we had steaming French bread right out of the oven. We greeted it with a big slab of soft butter in a pie tin and stood around the wooden work counter as we ate. It was amazing.

Easy French Bread

4 tsp. quick rising yeast

1⅓ cups warm water

1½ teaspoons salt

3 cups bread or all purpose flour

olive oil

cornmeal

Place water in a mixing bowl and sprinkle with yeast. Mix with a dough hook or a wooden spoon until dissolved. Allow to stand for about 10 minutes. Add flour and salt. Mix until all the flour is incorporated, scraping down the sides of the bowl once. The mixture will not be uniform. Remove the dough hook and leave the dough in the bowl, covered with a clean towel, in a warm place for about 1 to 2½ hours, depending on the time of year and temperature in your kitchen. Most of the time 1½ hours is perfect, but it will need less time on a very hot summer day and more time in the winter months. The dough should increase in volume 3 times.

Remove the towel and cover the bowl with plastic wrap. Place the dough in the refrigerator for 6 to 24 hours.

Prepare the French bread pans by lightly coating them with olive oil and a sprinkling of cornmeal. If you are concerned about the dough sticking, omit the oil and place parchment paper on the pan before sprinkling it with cornmeal.

Remove the dough from the bowl and divide it in two. Roll out each piece to about 6 by 10-inches. Roll up starting with one of the two long edges. (The dough will not be a perfect rectangle, it will likely be more like a trapezoid. Start rolling from whichever long side is a little shorter) Pinch the edges together and place seam down in the prepared pans.

Drape the loaves with a towel and allow to rise to about ¾ the size of fully baked bread for 1½ to 2 hours, again depending on the temperature in the room.

Place the pizza stone in the oven and preheat to 450°F about half an hour before you are ready to bake the bread. Just before baking, score the loaves at angles 4 or 5 times across the top. Spray the loaves a few times with water just before baking. Spray the bread with water again after the bread has been baking for 5 minutes and then again after another 5 minutes. Bake for a total of 15 to 18 minutes, turning the pans in the oven if necessary for even baking. You should be able to remove the bread from the pans right after baking. Allow to cool for at least 10 minutes before slicing.

Olive Rosemary Bread: Before rolling up, brush lightly with olive oil and sprinkle with sliced Kalamata olives and fresh rosemary. Roll up the dough and continue with instructions for final rise and bake.

Pain au Chocolat: Before rolling up the bread, place small chunks of chocolate near the inner edge. Roll up so that the chocolate will be in the center of the loaf. Continue with the instructions for the final rise and bake.

Whole Wheat French Bread: Substitute 1 cup of whole wheat flour for 1 cup of bread flour. Allow loaves to rise about 2½ hours or until close to full size before baking.

Cookies, Bars & Truffles

Chocolate Chunk Cookies [page 152],
Chocolate Chip Oatmeal Cookies [page 151],
and Coconut Macaroons [page 150]

Baking Pure & Simple

Cookies, Bars & Truffles

Coconut Macaroons

We used to sneak these right off the pans in Culinary school. Coconut Macaroons are pictured on page 148.

⅔ cup egg whites (approximately 4 whites)
1¾ cups sugar
½ teaspoon salt
2 teaspoons vanilla
⅓ cup flour or rice flour
1 pound unsweetened macaroon coconut*

parchment paper

Preheat oven to 350°F. In a large stainless steel bowl, whisk together egg whites, sugar, salt and vanilla. Stir in flour and coconut and place the bowl over a pan of simmering water. Stir often with a wooden spoon just until mixture is warm to the touch. Spoon or scoop onto pans lined with parchment paper since the cookies will stick to regular non-stick pans. If necessary, reshape the cookies after scooping. Wet your fingers in cool water first to keep the coconut mixture from sticking to your hands. Bake for 10 to 13 minutes. Cool slightly on the pan before removing to cooling racks.

If desired, dip the bottoms of fully cooled macaroons in melted semisweet chocolate and place on trays lined with parchment paper. Allow the chocolate to harden before serving or storing. Makes 4 dozen.

*If substituting sweetened coconut, reduce the sugar to 1¼ cups.

Chocolate Chip Oatmeal Cookies

Pictured on page 148.

1 cup unsalted butter, room temperature
1 cup sugar
1 cup brown sugar
2 eggs
2 teaspoons vanilla
1 teaspoon baking soda dissolved in 2 teaspoons hot water
1½ cups whole wheat or spelt flour
1 cup flour
1 teaspoon cinnamon (optional)
1 teaspoon salt
2 cups oatmeal
1 to 2 cups semi-sweet chocolate chips or chunks
1 cup walnuts or pecans, chopped
1 cup dried cherries (optional)

Preheat oven to 350°F. Cream butter and sugars. Add eggs and vanilla and continue to cream for a few minutes longer. Add the baking soda dissolved in hot water. Combine dry ingredients and add. Mix until just blended. Stir in oats, chips, nuts and dried cherries. Drop by tablespoons on a non-stick baking sheet. Bake for 12 to15 minutes. Makes 3 dozen.

The "Earthy Cookie" Gluten-Free Version: Substitute ½ cup almond flour and 2½ cups Gluten-Free Baking Mix (page 8) for the flours. Add ½ cup more oatmeal.

Maple Syrup Version: Substitute maple syrup for the (white) sugar. Reduce to one egg. Increase oatmeal to 3 cups.

White Chocolate Macadamia Nut Cookies: Substitute white chocolate chunks for the chocolate chunks and macadamia nuts for the walnuts or pecans. Get crazy and substitute shredded coconut for the dried cherries if you would like or leave them out all together.

Chocolate Chocolate Chunk Cookies

These cookies make great ice cream sandwiches. Any flavor ice cream will do. *Pictured on page 148.*

3½ tablespoons vegetable oil
10½ tablespoons cocoa
1 cup unsalted butter, room temperature
1¼ cups firmly packed brown sugar
1 cup sugar
2 eggs
2 teaspoons vanilla
2¼ cups flour
1 teaspoon salt
2 teaspoons baking soda
1 pound semisweet chocolate chunks
1½ cups walnuts or pecans, chopped

Heat vegetable oil over very low heat, remove from heat and stir in cocoa. Cool. Cream butter and sugars. Add eggs and vanilla. Combine flour, salt and soda. Add melted chocolate to creamed mixture and blend. Add dry ingredients, mixing just until combined. Add chocolate chunks and walnuts. Refrigerate for 2 hours or overnight.

Preheat oven to 350°F. Drop by heaping tablespoon on to non-stick cookie sheet. Bake for 11 to 13 minutes. Makes about 4 dozen.

Oatmeal Chocolate Chocolate Chunk Cookies: Reduce flour by ¼ cup and add 2 cups of oatmeal.

Oatmeal Raisin Cookies

1 cup unsalted butter, room temperature
¾ cup maple syrup
1 to 1¼ cups brown sugar
1 egg
2 teaspoons vanilla
2½ cups flour
2 teaspoons baking soda
1 teaspoon cinnamon
¼ teaspoon nutmeg
1 teaspoon salt
3 cups oatmeal
2 cups raisins, golden or regular
1 cup walnuts, chopped

2 cups oatmeal for rolling cookies in just prior to baking

Preheat oven to 350°F. Cream butter, maple syrup and brown sugar. Add egg and vanilla and continue to cream a few minutes longer, scraping down the sides several times. Combine flour, soda, cinnamon, nutmeg and salt and add to creamed mixture. Mix until just blended. Stir in oats, raisins and nuts. Roll into 1-inch balls, then roll in the additional oats, place on a non-stick baking sheet and flatten slightly. Bake for 12 to 15 minutes. Makes 3 to 4 dozen.

Maple Oatmeal Nut Cookies

Every now and then I take a break from sugar. I find I still need something that is a little sweet. These cookies are good at satisfying my baking needs and cravings during these health conscious moments.

1 cup unsalted butter, room temperature
1½ cups maple syrup
1 egg
2 teaspoons vanilla
2 cups whole wheat or spelt flour
½ cup ground flaxseed
2 teaspoons baking soda
1 teaspoon cinnamon
½ teaspoon nutmeg
1 teaspoon salt
3 cups oatmeal
1 cup walnuts, chopped

1 cup oatmeal for rolling cookies in just prior to baking

Preheat oven to 350°F. Cream butter and maple syrup. Add egg and vanilla and continue to cream a few minutes longer, scraping down the sides several times. Combine dry ingredients and add to creamed mixture. Mix until just blended. Stir in oats and nuts. Roll into 1-inch balls, then roll in the additional oats and place on a non-stick baking sheet and flatten slightly. Bake for 12 to 15 minutes. Makes 4 dozen.

Peanut Butter Granola Cookies

½ cup unsalted butter, room temperature
1 cup maple syrup
1 cup peanut butter, no sugar added, chunky
1 egg
1 teaspoon vanilla
1 cup whole wheat or spelt flour
2 teaspoons baking soda
¼ teaspoon salt
4 cups granola

Preheat oven to 350°F. Cream butter, maple syrup and peanut butter. Add egg and vanilla. Combine flour, baking soda and salt and add to creamed mixture. Mix until blended. Stir in granola. Place by heaping tablespoons on a baking sheet. Bake for 10 to 12 minutes. Makes 3 dozen.

This recipe comes from the kitchen of my childhood friend's mother. As kids, Carolyn and I would spend hours decorating cookies for the holidays, then package them up and distribute them to the neighbors. No one made cookies like Carolyn's mom.

Iced Butter Cookies

1 cup unsalted butter
1 cup sugar
2 eggs
1 teaspoon vanilla
1 teaspoon baking soda
¼ cup half and half
4 cups flour
¼ teaspoon salt

Butter Cookie Icing

Stir together 1 cup sifted powdered sugar, 2 to 3 teaspoons milk, ½ teaspoon vanilla and a few drops of food coloring as needed. Adjust with milk or powdered sugar to desired consistency.

Cream butter and sugar. Add eggs and vanilla. Continue creaming. Dissolve baking soda in half and half. Add to the creamed mixture. Sift flour and salt, add and mix. Chill dough for a few hours. Preheat oven to 350°F. Roll dough to ¼-inch thickness. Cut with cookie cutters. Bake for 8 to 10 minutes. Cool. Ice and decorate with sprinkles. Makes 5 dozen.

Soft Molasses Cookies with Crystallized Ginger [page 159], January Cookies [161] and Peanut Butter Cookies [page 160]

Soft Molasses Cookies with Crystallized Ginger

1 cup unsalted butter, room temperature
1 cup brown sugar (dark brown works best)
1 cup molasses
3½ cups flour
2 teaspoons cinnamon
2 teaspoons ground ginger
1 teaspoon ground cloves
½ teaspoon salt
2 teaspoons baking soda
2 teaspoons hot water
½ cup crystallized ginger, chopped
1 cup Turbinado sugar

Preheat oven to 325°F. Cream butter and brown sugar. Add molasses. Sift flour with spices and salt. Dissolve baking soda in hot water. Add half the flour mixture to the butter and sugar and mix. Add the dissolved baking soda and mix. Add the remaining flour mixture and mix just until combined. Add crystallized ginger. Roll into 1¼-inch balls. Roll balls in Turbinado sugar and place on cookie sheets. Bake for 8 to 12 minutes. Makes 4 dozen.

Molasses Oatmeal Raisin Cookies: Reduce flour by ½ cup and omit crystallized ginger. Add 1 cup golden raisins and 2 cups oatmeal. Bake for 14 to 15 minutes. Makes 5 dozen.

Peanut Butter Cookies

1 cup shortening
¾ cup sugar
1 cup brown sugar
2 eggs
1 teaspoon vanilla
1 cup peanut butter, crunchy or smooth
3 cups flour
2 teaspoon baking soda
½ teaspoon salt

Classic peanut butter cookies are still a favorite. At Christmas I make them with chocolate drops on top and my sister trades her Corn Flake Wreaths with my other sister for them. These cookies are pictured on page 158.

½ cup additional sugar for rolling cookies in before baking

Preheat oven to 375°F. Cream shortening and sugars. Add eggs and vanilla and continue to cream until light and fluffy. Stir in peanut butter. Sift flour, soda and salt and add to the mixture. Roll dough into 1½-inch balls and roll them in sugar. Place on a non-stick pan and flatten in a crisscross pattern with a fork dipped in sugar. Bake for 10 to 13 minutes. Cool on the pan a few minutes, then transfer to racks. Makes 3 dozen.

January Cookies

After all the holiday cookie baking in December, I always have leftover coconut, corn flakes, nuts and dried fruit around. I added them to this simple cookie recipe, originally from my grandma Gert, to create a winter favorite. These cookies are pictured on page 158.

1 cup unsalted butter, melted
2 cups brown sugar
2 eggs
2 cups flour
1 teaspoon soda
½ teaspoon salt
¼ teaspoon nutmeg
2 cups oatmeal
1 cup corn flakes, slightly crushed
1 to 1½ cups raisins or chopped dates
1 to 1½ cups chopped walnuts
1 to 1½ cups shredded coconut

Preheat oven to 350°F. Add melted butter to sugar, add eggs and mix. Sift flour, soda, salt and nutmeg together and add to the mixture. Add oatmeal, corn flakes, raisins or dates, nuts and coconut. Mix together. Roll into 1½-inch balls and flatten before placing on non-stick cookie sheets. Bake for 12 to 15 minutes. Makes 3 dozen.

Honey Almond Shortbread [page 180], Lemon Bars with Coconut Crust [page 184], Coconut Macaroons [page 150], Brownies [page 163], and Rasberry Rhapsody Bars [page 65]

Brownies

1 cup unsalted butter
¾ cup cocoa
2 cups sugar
4 eggs
1 teaspoon vanilla
1 cup flour
1 teaspoon baking powder
1 teaspoon salt
1 cup walnuts, chopped
1 cup semisweet chocolate chunks or chips

Preheat oven to 350°F. Melt butter over low heat in a heavy bottom saucepan. Remove from heat and add cocoa, then stir in sugar. Stir in eggs and vanilla. Add flour, baking powder and salt and stir to combine. Add nuts and chocolate chunks. Bake in a greased 13 by 9-inch baking pan for 27 to 30 minutes. Cool at least 1 hour before cutting. Cool completely before serving. Makes 2 dozen large or 4 dozen miniature brownies.

Cream Cheese Brownies: Cream together 4 tablespoons unsalted butter, 8 ounces cream cheese, ½ cup sugar, 1 teaspoon vanilla, 2 eggs and 2 tablespoons flour. Drop by dollops onto the brownie batter in the baking pan and swirl through before baking.

Peanut Butter Brownies: Omit walnuts. Cream together 1½ cups peanut butter, 1 cup powdered sugar, 1 teaspoon vanilla and 1 egg. Drop by dollops onto the brownie batter in the baking pan and swirl through before baking.

Motivated by my love of chocolate, at a young age I was determined to come up with a recipe for brownies which could satisfy my sweet tooth. I have been making these brownies the same way since I was 13 years old.

Chocolate Chip Peanut Butter Oatmeal Cookies

1 cup unsalted butter, room temperature
¾ cup sugar
1 cup brown sugar
1 cup peanut butter, chunky is best
2 eggs
1 teaspoon vanilla
1½ cups flour
2 teaspoons baking soda
1 teaspoon salt
2 cups oatmeal
2 cups milk chocolate chips

Preheat oven to 350°F. Cream butter, sugars and peanut butter. Add eggs and vanilla. Sift dry ingredients and add to creamed mixture. Mix until blended. Stir in oats and chips. Roll into 1½-inch balls and place on a non-stick baking sheet. Bake for 12 to 15 minutes. Makes 3 to 4 dozen.

These are vegan and contain no refined sugar but they are dangerously delicious.

Homemade Granola Bars

¾ cup peanut or almond butter, no sugar added
½ cup maple syrup
½ cup almond flour (finely ground almonds)
6 cups granola
1 cup raisins, dried cherries or coconut

Preheat oven to 350°F. Combine maple syrup, peanut butter and almond flour in the bowl of an electric mixer until blended. Add remaining ingredients. Mix until combined and sticky. Place the mixture into a 13 by 9-inch pan. Cut a piece of parchment paper into a 13 by 9-inch rectangle. Place the parchment paper over the top of the granola mixture and press very firmly with your hands until the mixture is flat and compact. Remove parchment paper. Using a bench scraper or a French knife, cut into 6 strips, about 2 inches wide each, and then cut once down the middle of the pan. You should have 12 bars, each 2 by 4 inches.

Bake in the pan for about 10 minutes or until they begin to brown just a little around the edges. Allow bars to cool for about 20 minutes in the pan. Using a bench scraper or a wide edged spatula remove the bars from the pan and turn them upside down individually on a baking sheet. Bake for another 10 to 12 minutes or until browned. Cool about 15 minutes before removing to cooling racks.

Note: Use a combination of peanut and almond butters if desired. My favorite ratio is twice as much almond butter as peanut butter, so ½ cup almond butter and ¼ cup peanut butter.

Hand Dipped Truffles

1 pound semi-sweet chocolate, chopped and divided in half
1 recipe Chocolate Truffle Ganache
1 recipe White Chocolate Truffle Ganache
Assorted nuts and liquors (see page 172 and 173)

Chocolate Truffle Ganache

10 ounces semi-sweet chocolate
1 cup heavy cream
hazelnut, orange, ginger or other liqueurs
¼ cup orange citron, small dice
¼ cup toasted hazelnuts, chopped
¼ cup crystallized ginger, finely chopped

Place cream in a heavy bottom saucepan and bring to a boil. Remove from heat immediately. Add chocolate. Whisk until smooth. Separate into three portions, each in a separate bowl. Add 2 tablespoons hazelnut liqueur and 1 tablespoon Cognac to one portion; 3 to 4 tablespoons orange flavored liqueur to another portion. Stir or whisk the liqueurs into the ganache and then chill the ganaches until set. Leave the other portion without a liqueur or, if you can find a ginger liqueur, try adding 2 to 3 tablespoons. Place each portion in a separate glass storage container, label and refrigerate until firm. Follow separate instructions for finishing truffles.

White Chocolate Truffle Ganache

½ pound white chocolate, chopped
3 tablespoons butter
¼ cup heavy cream
½ teaspoon lemon zest or 1 tablespoon brandy
¼ cup lemon citron, small dice for garnish

In a medium saucepan bring cream just to a boil and then add the butter. Reduce heat to medium. As soon as the butter has melted remove the pan from the heat. Add white chocolate and whisk until the mixture comes together. Add lemon zest or brandy. If desired, divide the ganache in half and add ¼ teaspoon lemon zest to one half and ½ tablespoon brandy to the other. Chill in the refrigerator several hours or overnight, until firm. Follow separate instructions for finishing truffles.

Finishing Truffles

Shaping Truffles: Once the ganaches are set, use a small scoop or spoon and portion out small portions about the size of a cherry. Next roll each small portion into a ¾-inch diameter ball. Embed a few tiny pieces of the orange citron into the orange liqueur truffles or a single small piece of the chopped crystallized ginger into the ginger liqueur or plain truffles. Shaping the truffles may be difficult and will be messy. You may have to smash the edges in to make the balls, then refrigerate them for a little while before rolling them in your hands again to get them into the desired spherical shape. Refrigerate thoroughly once they are the right shape.

Tempering Chocolate: Work with the divided chocolate in two batches. Set aside one half until the first batch is used up. Melt ¾ of one half of the chopped chocolate in a medium-size metal bowl over simmering water. When the chocolate is melted, remove it from the simmering water. Stir in the remaining ¼ of the chopped chocolate from this half into the melted chocolate until it is smooth. Test the temperature of the chocolate by using a small spoon and bringing a small amount of chocolate to just below your bottom lip, touching it to your skin. If it feels cool then the chocolate is at the right temperature. If the chocolate is too warm add a little more chopped chocolate and stir it in. Repeat the process with the other half of the chocolate using a clean metal bowl after you use up the first batch of tempered chocolate.

Enrobing Truffles: Line a few sheet pans with parchment paper. Begin enrobing truffles using 2 forks. One at a time dip each well-chilled ball of ganache into the melted chocolate and then retrieve it with one fork and use the other to scrape the chocolate from the bottom of the fork holding the truffle. Place the truffle on a half sheet pan lined with parchment paper. Using the back of the second fork hold the truffle in place on the parchment as you slide the other fork out from beneath. There may be some wisps of chocolate which trail off from the tines of the fork near the bottom of the truffle. You should be able to break these off later or you can try to smooth them gently back into the chocolate coating.

The idea behind tempering chocolate is to bring all the elements in the chocolate to the same temperature before it hardens. The worst that can happen is that some of your truffles will be a little bit streaked on the outside when the chocolate hardens. It may take a few trials to get it just right, but your friends will not mind if you experiment on them. Your truffles should begin to harden in just a few minutes if the chocolate is tempered correctly. When set, they should have a crispness when you bite into them and the chocolate should be free of streaks. Practice, practice, practice.....everyone will love it that you are practicing.

Holiday Cookie Distribution

Early in the season, often right after Halloween, I check out the craft or dollar stores for medium-sized tins. I usually get tins which are 6" to 7" in diameter and about 3" tall. These tins hold 2 dozen holiday cookies very nicely. I also get some colored tissue paper, tiny candy holders, mini air tight snack bags and bubble wrap since I have to mail a few of my boxes.

When it is time to package the cookies, I make up many of the cookie tins at the same time, lining each container with some tissue paper and packing the cookies from the sturdiest, such as Honey Almond Shortbreads and Ginger Molasses Cookies on the bottom to the most fragile and decorative, say the Corn Flake Wreaths and the Orange Almond Macaroons, on top. I put the Rum Balls and Mexican Wedding Cakes into the small candy holders and if I am sending the tins, I also put them in the mini storage bags. I have found that these tins fit perfectly into the standard air tight freezer bag. Once all the tins are made up I can place each one into a gallon freezer bag, and store them in the freezer until they need to be distributed. The cookies will thaw out in a few hours, so you just need to pull the tin out the morning of the day you plan to give it.

I log how many cookies each batch makes in my spreadsheet and from that I figure out how many cookies I can put in each box and have enough leftover to make assortment trays for my work, my family and any other gatherings. It works out to about 1-3 of each type of cookie per tin for about 24 tins, plus about 3-4 cookies each for each of the 4 trays. I keep track of who gets cookies year after year so I don't forget anyone. As you can imagine, the list grows annually. I try to add new cookies once in a while, to keep up with the increasing number of necessary tins.

Honey Almond Shortbreads

The best part about making Honey Almond Shortbreads is that when you trim the edges before you cut out the bars then you have a whole bunch of edges leftover. Mix them with soft vanilla ice cream and refreeze it. It's the best.

Crust:

1⅓ cups unsalted butter, room temperature
¾ cup sugar
1 egg
1 teaspoon vanilla
3½ cups flour

Topping:

1½ cups unsalted butter
1¾ cups sugar
⅔ cup honey
1½ pounds sliced almonds

Preheat oven to 350°F.

Crust: Cream butter and sugar. Add egg and vanilla. Add flour to the mixture and blend until combined. Press into a 13 by 18 by ¾-inches baking pan and prick with a fork. This is the size of a half sheet pan in a commercial kitchen. Bake for 12 to 15 minutes until slightly brown around the edges. Check during baking and deflate any puffs with a fork. Remove from oven and set aside. You could also divide the dough between two 9x13-inch pans.

Topping: Meanwhile, melt butter with sugar and honey. Add almonds and stir until coated. Spread over the partially baked shortbread crust. Continue baking until golden brown and bubbly another 15 to 20 minutes. Cool to room temperature. Trim about ½-inch around each side. Cut the rest into rectangles or triangles after cooling for about 45 minutes but before completely cool. If desired, drizzle with melted chocolate. Makes 6 dozen.

Cinnamon Stars

½ cup unsalted butter, room temperature
1 cup sugar
3 egg yolks
2 tablespoons milk
2 cups flour
2 teaspoons cinnamon
½ teaspoon baking powder
½ teaspoon salt

Cream butter and sugar. Add egg yolks, then milk and combine. Sift flour, cinnamon, baking powder and salt. Add to creamed mixture and mix until just combined. Chill for 3 hours.

Preheat oven to 350°F. Roll out approximately ⅜-inch thickness. Cut with star shaped cookie cutters. Bake for 8 to 10 minutes. Makes 4 dozen.

Orange Almond Macaroons

[illegible] egg [illegible]
2 cups powdered sugar, sifted
2¾ cups ground almonds
3 cups unsweetened coconut
¼ cup orange zest (zest of 2 oranges)
2 tablespoons orange liqueur

2 cups semi-sweet chocolate, melted

Preheat oven to 350°F. Whip whites, adding powdered sugar slowly. Once whites are stiff, gently fold in nuts, coconut, orange zest and orange liqueur. Drop by rounded tablespoons onto non-stick trays. Bake for 9 to 10 minutes.

When cool, dip the bottom half of each cookie in melted chocolate and place on a tray lined with parchment paper. Drizzle the tops with melted chocolate to finish. Allow the chocolate to harden before serving or storing. Makes 4 to 5 dozen.

Almond Cookies

1½ cups unsalted butter, room temperature
1½ cups sugar
3 egg yolks
2 teaspoons almond extract
¼ cup water
5 cups flour
2 teaspoons baking powder
½ teaspoon salt

1 cup sugar for rolling cookies in before baking
1 cup whole raw almonds

Preheat oven to 350°F. Cream butter and sugar. Add egg yolks, almond extract and water to creamed mixture. Sift flour, baking powder and salt and add to mixture. Blend until combined. Shape dough into 1¼-inch balls, roll in sugar and place on a non-stick cookie sheet. Press to flatten with the flat bottom of a short wide glass dipped in sugar. Press a whole almond into the center of each cookie. Bake for 12 to 14 minutes. Makes 5 dozen.

Lemon Bars with Coconut Crust

¾ cup unsalted butter
⅜ cup sugar
⅛ teaspoon salt
1½ cups flour
2 cups unsweetened coconut
¾ tablespoon lemon rind, grated

5 eggs
1⅔ cups sugar
½ cup lemon juice
1 tablespoon lemon rind, grated
¾ tablespoon flour
A pinch of salt

½ cup powdered sugar for dusting

Crust: Preheat oven to 350°F. Cream butter and sugar. Add salt and flour and mix. Add coconut and lemon rind and mix just until blended. Press evenly into the bottom of a 13 by 9-inch non-stick baking pan. Use a rolling pin to evenly flatten the surface. Bake for 10 minutes. Remove from oven if the topping is not yet ready.

Topping: While the crust is baking, blend the eggs and sugar until just mixed. Add the lemon juice, rind, flour and salt and mix until just combined. Place the crust in the oven with the shelf pulled out slightly but make sure it is secure and level. Carefully and evenly pour the lemon juice mixture over the top of the partially baked crust. Slowly push the oven shelf back into place before closing the oven door. Bake for 20 minutes or until firm.

Allow to cool completely before cutting. Trim away edges if desired. Dust with powdered sugar before serving. Makes 3 dozen.

Note: The edges are great chopped up and sprinkled over vanilla ice cream.

Thumbprint Cookies

1½ cups unsalted butter, room temperature
1½ cups sugar
4 egg yolks
1 teaspoon vanilla
½ teaspoon almond extract
4 cups flour
1 teaspoon salt
1 to 2 egg whites, slightly beaten
2 cups chopped walnuts
assorted jams and jellies

I think the best preserves to use in these cookies are orange marmalade or raspberry jam but feel free to experiment. I like to have a large variety so I usually also include strawberry preserves and grape jelly, too.

Preheat oven to 350°F. Cream butter and sugar until light and fluffy. Add egg yolks and vanilla and almond extract and continue beating. Sift flour and salt. Add to creamed mixture until combined. Roll dough into 1-inch balls. Dip in egg whites, then roll in walnuts. Place on cookie sheets and make an indentation in the center with your finger. Bake for 13 to 16 minutes.

While still warm fill the center depression with about half a teaspoon of jam or jelly from a small spoon. Remove from trays to racks to cool. Makes 5 to 6 dozen.

Mexican Wedding Cookies

4 cups flour
4 cups pecans, finely chopped
½ cup sugar
[illegible] salt

2 cups unsalted butter, room temperature
2 to 3 cups powdered sugar

Combine flour, pecans, sugar, salt and vanilla. Work in butter by hand until mixture is uniform. Chill for several hours.

Preheat oven to 375°F. Roll into 1-inch balls and bake for 9 to 12 minutes. Cool completely before rolling in powdered sugar. Just before serving roll in powdered sugar again. Makes 4 dozen.

Viennese Cookies

2 cups unsalted butter, room temperature
1 cup powdered sugar
½ teaspoon almond extract
2 teaspoons vanilla
4 cups flour
2 cups ground pecans or walnuts
¼ teaspoon salt

1 cup semi-sweet chocolate, melted

Cream butter, powdered sugar, almond extract and vanilla. Mix flour and ground nuts with salt. Combine with butter mixture and knead slightly until blended. Chill for several hours.

Preheat oven to 375°F. Shape into crescents about 3 inches long. Bake for 10 to 14 minutes. Drizzle with melted chocolate after cooling. Allow chocolate to harden before serving or storing. Makes 5 dozen.

Rum Balls

2½ cups golden raisins
1 cup rum, dark, vanilla or spiced
1½ tablespoons unsalted butter
1½ tablespoons cocoa
11½ ounces semi-sweet chocolate chips or chunks
½ cup corn syrup
1½ cup ground pecans
12 ounces vanilla wafers, finely ground in the food processor

1 cup cocoa for coating finished rum balls

Place raisins into a large bowl and add rum. Stir to mix and set aside. Melt butter in the top of a double boiler over gently simmering water. Add the 1½ tablespoons cocoa and the chocolate and stir with a wooden spoon until melted; remove from heat. Add the corn syrup to the chocolate mixture. Add the pecans and ground vanilla wafers to the soaked raisins then stir into the chocolate mixture. Chill a few hours or over night. Shape into ¾" balls and roll in cocoa. Makes 5 dozen.

Basler Brunsli

5 ounces [illegible]
3¾ cups powdered sugar
6 egg whites
1 tablespoon cinnamon
4½ cups ground pecans or almonds
1 tablespoon lemon zest, grated

Preheat oven to 325°F. Melt chocolate over very low heat. Remove from heat and whisk in the powdered sugar and egg whites until combined. Stir in the cinnamon, nuts and lemon zest. Drop by tablespoons full onto non-stick cookie sheets. Bake for 14 to 15 minutes. Cool slightly before removing from trays to cooling racks. Makes 5 dozen.

Ginger Molasses Cookies

This dough may also be rolled out and cut into gingerbread people or other holiday shapes.

½ cup unsalted butter, room temperature
1 cup brown sugar
2 eggs
¾ cup molasses
4½ cups flour
½ teaspoon allspice
½ teaspoon cinnamon
½ teaspoon ground ginger
½ teaspoon ground cloves
½ teaspoon salt
1½ teaspoon baking soda

1 cup sugar for rolling cookies in before baking.

Cream butter and brown sugar. Add eggs one at a time, mixing until incorporated and stopping to scrape down the sides of the bowl as needed. Add molasses and mix. Sift flour with spices, salt and soda. Add to creamed mixture just until combined to form a stiff dough. Chill for several hours.

Preheat oven to 350°F. Roll into 1-inch balls. Roll balls in sugar and place on non-stick cookie sheets. Press to flatten with the bottom of a short wide glass dipped in sugar. Bake for 10 to 12 minutes. Makes 6 dozen.

Cherry Winks

⅓ cup [illegible]
½ cup sugar
1 egg
1 teaspoon vanilla
1⅛ cups flour
¼ teaspoon salt
¼ teaspoon baking soda
½ teaspoon baking powder
1½ cups crushed corn flakes
1½ dozen maraschino cherries, cut in half

Preheat oven to 350°F. Cream shortening and sugar. Add egg and vanilla. Combine flour, salt, baking soda and powder. Add to creamed mixture and blend until combined. Roll into 1-inch balls and then roll in crushed corn flakes. Place on a non-stick cookie sheet and press each cookie down in the center. Place half a maraschino cherry, cut side down, in the center of each cookie. Bake for 10 to 12 minutes. Makes 3 dozen.

Corn Flake Wreaths

¾ cups unsalted butter
21 ounces miniature marshmallows
8 cups corn flakes
green food coloring
red hot dots
vegetable shortening to grease your hands

It is best to make Corn Flake Wreaths with a friend. The red hots must be placed on the wreaths before they cool. One person shapes the wreaths while the other decorates them.

Melt butter and marshmallows slowly over very low heat. Stir until completely melted and uniform consistency. Remove from heat. Add green food coloring to desired shade. Add corn flakes and stir with a wooden spoon until mixed. Shape into wreaths with greased hands and place on greased trays or greased parchment paper. Decorate with 3 to 5 red hot dots immediately. Makes 4 dozen.

D

E

F

G

H

I

J

K

L